ROUTLEDGE LIBRARY EDITIONS:
BANKING & FINANCE

THE EXPORT OF CAPITAL FROM BRITAIN 1870–1914

THE EXPORT OF CAPITAL FROM BRITAIN 1870–1914

Edited with an introduction by
A. R. HALL

Volume 16

Routledge
Taylor & Francis Group
LONDON AND NEW YORK

First published in 1968

This edition first published in 2012
by Routledge
2 Park Square, Milton Park, Abingdon, Oxon, OX14 4RN

Simultaneously published in the USA and Canada
by Routledge
711 Third Avenue, New York, NY 10017

Routledge is an imprint of the Taylor & Francis Group, an informa business

British Library Cataloguing in Publication Data
A catalogue record for this book is available from the British Library

ISBN: 978-0-415-52086-7 (Set)
eISBN: 978-0-203-10819-2 (Set)
ISBN: 978-0-415-53893-0 (Volume 16)
eISBN: 978-0-203-10871-0 (Volume 16)

Publisher's Note
The publisher has gone to great lengths to ensure the quality of this reprint but
points out that some imperfections in the original copies may be apparent.

Disclaimer
The publisher has made every effort to trace copyright holders and would
welcome correspondence from those they have been unable to trace.

Printed and bound by CPI Group (UK) Ltd, Croydon, CR0 4YY

The Export of Capital from Britain 1870–1914

edited with an introduction by

A. R. HALL

METHUEN & CO LTD
11 NEW FETTER LANE LONDON EC4

First published 1968 by Methuen & Co Ltd
Introduction © 1968 by A. R. Hall
Printed in Great Britain by
Richard Clay (The Chaucer Press), Ltd,
Bungay, Suffolk

Distributed in the U.S.A.
by Barnes & Noble Inc.

Contents

Preface

As the international economy grinds its way through the twentieth century the experience of the generations before 1914 can be seen for what it really was – the most explosive phase in the world's economic development to date. It is like moving away from a mountain range: the foothills fade in the perspective given by distance, revealing the peaks in their true scale. Such expansion came in response to a unique combination of historical circumstances – how much so we have cause to ponder upon at the present time – and many of its facets were as unique individually as was the process as a whole. The present volume is concerned only with one aspect of this process, the export of capital, but later contributions will cover related themes.

Empty continents awaiting settlement, with virgin lands able to pour out an unprecedented stream of primary products, foodstuffs, minerals, and other raw materials, set the context. The great migration from Europe to these population-hungry countries, the ocean shipping and the railways to open up the interiors of great land masses gave the necessary flows of people and materials. Foreign investment, and its interaction with the surges of economic activity in the home country, provides the theme for this book, but such capital flows themselves fitted into a complex set of interactions which can be seen as underpinning the whole process of expanding the international economy. Some links were one-to-one, with the provision of the capital goods embodied in the export of capital – over 40 per cent of capital exported from Britain financed railway investment overseas – and directly stimulated British export industries supplying these products, particularly up to the 1870s. Even where direct links to the export industries are not traceable, capital exports joined a complicated sequence of relationships which, as surely if less directly, served the expansion of the international economy. With

Britain the most important trading and shipping country in the world, running a very large, and increasing, surplus on her balance of payments (though not on her balance of trade) constraint might have come from a chronic 'sterling gap'. The open ports of a free-trade economy (indeed, the rising deficit on its balance of trade), a multilateral payments system based on the international gold standard, and the export of capital were pillars guarding the gate of international liquidity. With the world painfully struggling into a second era of free trade – even if it is now to be absolutely free trade only within economic blocs and just lower tariffs between the blocs – we are in a better position to see how these relationships buttressed each other. Present curbs against foreign investment point the same moral. Before 1914, without official manipulation, a free market economy was investing abroad in some years at a much greater rate than it was investing at home, to the extent of 7 per cent of its national income. In the present United Nations 'Development Decade', despite all efforts of government and international agency lending, the club of industrial nations has failed to meet its original ambition of investing just 1 per cent of their national incomes in the developing world.

In one short volume many implications of the export of capital, which raise debates of their own, have to be omitted. Dr Hall has set out the terms in which the mechanisms of the foreign investment must be analysed. The varied results – upon present-day developing countries as well as the United States and the 'white' Dominions which received the lion's share of British capital – await discussion; as also does the thesis that such capital could more profitably have been employed at home, whether in 'social overhead capital' investment – there were slums enough to be rebuilt – or in industries old and new needing, we are told, a higher rate of investment than they received.

PETER MATHIAS

Acknowledgements

The editor and publishers wish to thank the following for permission to reproduce the articles listed below:

Cambridge University Press for 'Investment in Canada, 1900–13', by Sir Alexander Cairncross (*Home and Foreign Investment, 1870–1913*, 1953); Dr A. G. Ford for 'Overseas Lending and Internal Fluctuations, 1870–1914' (*The Yorkshire Bulletin*, May 1965); The Economic History Association for 'Fluctuations in House-Building in Britain and the United States in the Nineteenth Century', by Professor H. J. Habakkuk (*The Journal of Economic History*, June 1962); Australian National University Press for 'Capital Imports and the Composition of Investment in a Borrowing Country', by Dr A. R. Hall (*The London Capital Market and Australia, 1870–1914*, 1963); Macmillan & Company Ltd for 'The Pattern of New British Portfolio Foreign Investment, 1865–1914', by Professor Matthew Simon (*Capital Movements and Economic Development*, 1967); Macmillan & Company Ltd and the International Economic Association for 'Migration and International Investment', by Professor Brinley Thomas (*The Economics of International Migration*, 1958); The Economic History Association for 'The Long Swing: Comparisons and Interactions Between British and American Balance of Payments, 1820–1913', by Dr J. G. Williamson (*The Journal of Economic History*, March 1962).

Editor's Introduction

It is roughly estimated that between 1870 and 1914 Britain's capital exports amounted to some £3,500 million. In relation to the price levels of the time and to the then size of its economy this diversion of British savings for use abroad is quite remarkable. Nothing comparable, in terms of proportions of resources devoted to overseas investment, had occurred before over any lengthy period. Nor has anything comparable occurred since then. Equally noteworthy in the light of post-1914 experience, this flow of resources abroad was almost entirely in response to market considerations. What was the nature of the world in which this process occurred? What were the market mechanisms that produced it?

A brief answer to the first question can only be given in very impressionistic terms. It leads naturally into a provisional answer to the second and runs roughly along the following lines. At some time between about 1840 and about 1870 the weight of Western European economic expansion, a compound of growing population, and increasing productivity, began to press against the limits of Western Europe's regional resources. This pressure began to make itself felt at a time when a large part of the earth's land surface was virtually unused. One symptom of this situation was the beginning of large-scale population movements into the world's vacant spaces. The exact timing of these movements was influenced by such events as the Irish potato famine, the political revolutions of 1848, and the discovery of the gold-mining eldorados of California and Australia. These same years also saw major cost reductions for long-distance transport both by land and by sea and felt the impact of the revolution in communications associated with the electric telegraph. Part cause, part effect of Europe's growing need for resources outside its own boundaries, the foundations were being laid for world markets in the major products of the earth, not merely for luxuries – furs, spices, and precious metals – but also for age-old necessities such as wheat and for the newer necessities of an industrial civilization – iron, coal, and the base metals.

If this were a work concerned with political history it would be natural to direct attention to the formation of national states in Europe in the years around about 1870 and concentrate on the political aspects associated with the next phase in the process of Europe's incorporation of the rest of the world into its economic sphere of influence. This would be a discussion of the 'age of imperialism'. In fact it is concerned with economic processes. While European nationalism abroad did have economic aspects and economic consequences they were not central to the changing pattern of the world's use of resources. Changes in it remained essentially a by-product of the maintenance of trends which had become evident in the previous thirty years or so. Compound economic growth in Europe required ever larger supplies of foodstuffs and raw materials. Partly as a result of the increased scale on which goods were being brought on to the world market, partly in order to make this increased movement of goods possible, the trend towards cheaper transport costs continued. Ships were increasingly made of iron and steel; they became larger, travelled faster, and used proportionately less fuel to carry a unit of goods any given distance. Railways, increasingly made of steel, spread across the continents of North America and Asia and penetrated farther and farther into South America, Africa, and Australasia. Along this ever-extending and increasingly efficient world transport system flowed an expanding volume of goods.

Both the scale on which this process occurred and the speed with which it took place were conditioned not merely by the rate of technical change in transport but also by international movements of the factors of production, labour, and capital. Under nineteenth-century conditions railway construction involved large-scale use of labour. More often than not, directly and indirectly, a significant proportion of the required labour was obtained from Europe. Equally important, part of the food, clothing, etc., and equipment required by this construction work force was supplied by Europe on deferred terms of payment. By consuming less of its foreign-earned income than it produced (i.e. by exporting capital), Europe enabled this process of expansion to be completed in a much shorter time than would otherwise have been possible.

The preceding account has emphasized the part played by railways in facilitating the flow of goods and services between Europe and the rest of the world and in stimulating the international movement of factors of production. This view of the process is nevertheless seriously incomplete. The exploitation of large areas of new land made possible by the new railway (and shipping) technology had other characteristics which have not yet been given sufficient attention. Because land was relatively cheap in the areas of recent settlement that were in the process of being opened up by railways it was initially brought into production with relatively little use of labour and other types of capital resources. A relatively small proportion of the growing population of these areas was directly involved in working the land. Instead the greater part of the population came to be concentrated in the ports and nodal transport centres of the new world. The widespread opening up of new land was thus associated with a higher degree of urbanization, in the sense of the proportion of the population contained in large cities, than was yet the case in Europe itself. This urban concentration in the areas of recent settlement, a by-product of their relative factor proportions under conditions of late nineteenth-century industrial technology, had at least as much significance in shaping the international flow of capital and labour as did the mere building of railways. In fact, as was recognized many years ago by Isard, the construction of railways and the building of cities in the areas of recent settlement should be regarded as a joint product.[1] It was this combined relationship, rather than either segment of it taken by itself, that provoked bursts of development which could only be sustained at a high rate and for long periods by the inflow of capital and labour from Europe on a large scale.

[1] W. Isard, 'Transport Development and Building Cycles', in *Quarterly Journal of Economics* (1942).

That the opening up of resources in the new areas proceeded by spasms and not as a smooth continuous process must probably be attributed to this railways-urbanization characteristic of the development process. Railway building involves long periods from the initial plan for a new railway system until the time when goods flow through that system on a scale sufficient to justify the original investment decision. Similarly the building of cities involves the construction of very long lived assets – roads, bridges, harbour facilities, office buildings, warehouses, houses, etc. The provision of one type of urban facility does not necessarily keep in step with the provision of the others. For these and other reasons, once conditions had arisen which favoured investment in railways-urbanization it was to be expected that the process of construction would continue for relatively long periods before declining returns on investment tended to bring it to a halt. During the period of expansion the length of leads and lags in the construction process was such that the economies experiencing one of these investment booms were relatively undisturbed by short-term fluctuations in inventories, harvest conditions, etc., and by those random shocks which are always occurring during any historical sequence of events.

When the developmental process reached the stage when diminishing returns on further new investment were becoming apparent the whole system became more vulnerable to the adverse influence of shorter term fluctuations and/or random shocks. Once these conditions combined to halt the investment boom the short-term depression that followed was likely to be an acute one. Throughout the period of depression output from the preceding burst of investment flowed on to the market in increasingly large quantities and in due course aggregate real income began to rise again. This process was furthered by the changing pattern of relative prices and costs which had been one aspect of the after-boom depression. In this situation profit opportunities opened up in avenues of investment that were less capital consuming than the railways-urbanization complex had been and which had, relatively speaking, been starved of capital during the previous boom. While recovery thus proceeded it was more restrained than in the earlier period and the whole economic system was more vulnerable to short-term adverse economic influences. Under these conditions it was to be expected that it would be a relatively lengthy period before the excess capacity of the boom in transport-urbanization was worked off and before there was a renewed appearance of high profit expectations in the heavily capital-using sectors of the economy. Not surprisingly, during these less capital intensive phases of development in the areas of recent settlement much greater reliance was placed on domestic savings and existing supplies of labour. There was an ebb tide in the long-term movement of capital and labour resources out of Europe.

The preceding analysis of the long period fluctuations in the opening up of the resources of the 'new world' has tended to proceed as though it were a self-contained process, one which depended simply on expected profit opportunities in the United States, Australia, the Argentine, etc. In fact, this emphasis arises simply as a result of expository convenience. At every stage in the process of long-term fluctuation conditions in Europe and the new world were intimately interconnected. At the level of trading relationships one country's exports were some other country's (countries') imports. Export prices plus freight, etc., charges were equal to import prices. The profit opportunities connected with a rise in export prices implied a favourable demand situation in the importing country. And so on. Partly, but not entirely, because there were flows of factors of production as well as flows of goods, changes in those sectors of the economy not directly related to international trade were also conditioned by influences external to the new world. In the short term, at each point of time when they occurred, inflows of capital and labour tended to lower the supply price of these factors below what they otherwise would have been. Once incorporated within the receiving economic system these labour and capital supplies altered domestic demand conditions. Both because of interest rate and wage rate effects and because of influences on aggregate demand the length of the process of expansion tended to be increased well beyond the period that would otherwise have been possible. Also important from this point of view was the absence of a balance of payments constraint so long as the inflow of capital occurred at an appropriate rate. The length of the spurts of expansion, most obviously in the case of 'small' economies such as Australia, the Argentine, and Canada but also true of the United States, was therefore not merely a function of the length of the period of construction of railways-urbanization and of its leads and lags but also of the availability *at the margin* of extra-national sources of labour and capital. The development of the world economy in the period 1870 to 1914 was not simply the consequence of resource exploitation possibilities at the perimeter, but of a complex set of interrelationships whereby conditions in Europe reacted on conditions in the areas of recent settlement.

In this rather roundabout way one has come at last to the subject indicated by the title of this work. While directly and indirectly the other major European countries were involved in this world-wide process of developing the earth's resources, none of them played quite the same role as Britain and in none of them are the effects of a major process of capital export on a large lending country under more or less competitive market conditions so readily apparent. Probably in the course of the 1850s Britain came to experience simultaneous major flows of capital and labour into the new world. Equally important, the flows of capital abroad came to match in size the amount of investment in domestic development. It is largely because the proportions of home and foreign investment were of this character that the subsequent pattern of British development in the period 1870 to 1914 so clearly reflects the ebbs and flows of the process of expansion in the areas of recent settlement. When the pull of a long investment boom in these areas made itself felt there was a flow of capital and labour resources abroad. While the outer rim of the world was digesting the consequences of one of these long booms British savings were used to exploit domestic investment opportunities.

This long-term inverse movement of British home and foreign investment, to which attention was first directed by

A. K. Cairncross, is an undisputed fact. It is the explanation of this pattern of relationships which is the subject of argument. Cairncross in his original exposition of the interplay of home and foreign investment emphasized the simultaneous movement of labour and capital abroad, their effects on wage and interest rates at home and abroad, and also the relative movement of British export and import prices (Britain's terms of trade). Since then there has been a continuous, though sporadic, debate on the nature of the causal mechanism. Some, notably Brinley Thomas, have accepted the general position of Cairncross but have discounted the independent influence of changes in Britain's terms of trade and have given greater weight than he did to the causal role of migration. Others, for example Williamson, have emphasized the central role of the United States and have tended to play down Britain's own contribution to the interacting process. Still others, for example Ford, have emphasized changes in Britain's willingness to lend abroad, both in the short and in the long term, as an essential ingredient of the sequence of events. Others again, notably Habakkuk, have reacted to the 'pull' hypothesis and have directed attention to the domestic ingredients in Britain's bursts of home investment. He (and also writers such as Lewis and O'Leary), has been somewhat sceptical that there was in fact a systematic set of interrelationships.[1]

As will be apparent from the earlier discussion the present writer does not accept the last mentioned view. Consider, for example, one way in which changes abroad must intimately have affected the British economy. In the course of the 1890s Britain embarked on one of its periodic domestic investment booms which, in a somewhat similar fashion to those which occurred abroad in earlier and later decades, was essentially a

[1] The works cited in this paragraph are: A. K. Cairncross, *Home and Foreign Investment 1870–1913* (Cambridge, 1953); B. Thomas, Chapter 3 below, *Migration and Economic Growth* (Cambridge, 1954), 'Wales and the Atlantic Economy', *Scottish Journal of Political Economy*, VI (1959), 'The Historical Record of International Capital Movements to 1913', in J. H. Adler (ed.) *Capital Movements and Economic Development* (London, 1967); J. G. Williamson, Chapter 4 below and *American Growth and the Balance of Payments 1820–1913* (North Carolina, 1964); H. J. Habakkuk, Chapter 6 below; P. J. O'Leary and W. A. Lewis, 'Secular Swings in Production and Trade', *The Manchester School* (May 1955).

boom involving a pronounced shift in the urbanization of Britain. Like the urban building booms abroad it was partly shaped by urban transport developments; like them it probably involved relatively large-scale investment in shops, offices, warehouses, houses, etc.; like them it was accompanied by migrations of labour to the cities. Among the particular ingredients in this complex of processes, as Habakkuk has rightly stressed, there undoubtedly were a number which should properly be described as 'domestic' in origin. It is nevertheless highly improbable that these purely domestic components were in themselves sufficient to account for the strength and duration of this particular boom. Among its important contributing factors must be included the decline in interest rates after 1890 and the dramatic cheapening of imported foodstuffs and raw materials in the early years of the 1890s. The first factor was one ingredient in improving the relative profitability of investment in domestic building in general and housing in particular. The second factor had a two-fold effect. The increase in real wages which it implied freed earnings at the margin for other uses of which one important one was housing. At the same time it implied strong competitive pressure on British rural industries and an additional 'push' on the rural population driving them into British towns at a time when emigration abroad was not in general an attractive proposition. All these processes which intimately affected the pricing, costing, demand, and location of domestic investment can properly be regarded as part of the consequences following upon the completion of one of the major bursts of investment overseas. It is unreasonable to dismiss these elements in the process, as Habakkuk does, as being 'of minor importance compared with domestic factors'.

On the other hand, in so far as Habakkuk was objecting to the view that conditions in the United States *determined* building fluctuations in Britain he was almost certainly correct. Such an hypothesis in the 1890s, or in the 1870s, just does not make sense. Why should a depression in one country, however big it may be, *create* a boom in some other country? Surely the co-existence of a boom in Britain and depression in the United

States in the middle 1870s and the 1890s implies that British domestic booms during these periods must have had some degree of internal logic of their own.

The argument of the two preceding paragraphs is not, as it might at first appear, internally inconsistent. That British domestic booms were significantly affected by events abroad and that they had important domestic determinants in their own right are not mutually exclusive statements. They merely imply that a plurality of causal processes was at work and that there was an inevitable degree of interdependence between different regions of the world economy. Thus it is also possible to argue that when major booms occurred in the areas of recent settlement they contained a large degree of 'self-determination' and also that they were significantly influenced by the willingness and ability of the British economy to adjust to conditions of strong oversea demand for labour and capital. The conclusion which follows from this twofold set of pro-positions is that what might be described as the central locus of economic stimulus within the world economy was not continuously located in any one region. It could and did shift from region to region among the areas of recent settlement and between those regions, regarded as a single entity, and Europe and within Europe to Britain in particular. Because long-lived investment booms, whether they were at home or abroad, tended to leave behind them a legacy of excess capacity in the heavily capital consuming sectors of the economy and because interconnected flows of capital and labour played an important part in them it seems reasonable to expect, as appears to have been the case, that under pre-1914 conditions there would be a regular alternation between Britain and abroad in that relative degree of economic independence that appears to be a characteristic of major investment booms centred on the provision of transport *cum* urban facilities.

Not only are there strong grounds for refusing to accept a single location source for these international fluctuations there are also strong reasons for rejecting any single-cause explanation of the economic dynamics of the process. The alternation of regional investment booms did not depend simply on changes in the expected rate of profit on new investment; it did not depend simply on the push of international labour flows; it did not depend simply on autonomous shifts in British willingness to lend; nor did it depend on any single price relationship such as the ratio of British export and import prices. On the contrary it depended on the complicated interplay of all these variables, and numerous others. Changes in any one of them reacted on the others but not in any simple way. The nature of the reaction to changes in any one ingredient was not always identical because the conjuncture of other factors when such changes occurred was not always the same. Simple mono-causal explanation such as those noted above, all of which have been subjected to more or less sophisticated statistical testing, are all doomed to be found wanting. Unfortunate though the fact may be for those who try to understand the detailed workings of the economic system, the way in which it works is very complicated. The mechanism governing the movements of British capital exports between 1870 and 1914 is no exception to this generalization.

The preceding discussion of British capital exports before 1914 and of the world scene in which they were an important factor has concentrated on the relationship between British home and foreign investment. This emphasis has arisen partly because this interrelationship appears to be central to an understanding of the mechanism governing much of the movement of British capital exports during these years and partly because this is the main aspect of the process that has been the subject of debate among economic historians. It is now time briefly to recognize that this central debate and the type of economic analysis which seems appropriate for an approximate understanding of the economic process whereby the regions of recent settlement were settled and incorporated into the world market gives at best a partial coverage of the complete phenomenon of British capital exports between 1870 and 1914.

As has already been obliquely indicated part of the flow of British capital abroad went to the densely settled areas of the ancient civilizations of Asia and into the still different areas of Africa and the Near East. In these areas, which received a relatively small but still significant share of the total outflow, the impact of capital exports was of a very different character to what it was in the areas of recent settlement. It was, for example, accompanied by European labour flows – essentially of managerial and key technical staff – of minor statistical importance. It did not as a general rule involve the opening up of essentially virgin land but tended to take place in economies in which land was in relatively short supply. The domestic labour force was not imbued with the same attitudes to work and leisure and did not possess the same types of technical skills as did that which was primarily involved in opening up the areas of recent settlement. For these reasons alone it is to be expected that the process of interaction between the borrowing countries and the lender would be, as they were, very different.

It also needs to be remembered that not all British capital exports (and certainly not all the capital exports of the other major European lending countries) flowed to 'underdeveloped' economies. At the opening of the period surveyed capital exports to Europe formed a significant proportion of total British capital exports. As is apparent from Jenks' *The Migration of British Capital to 1875* this was not a new phenomenon. Similarly in the years immediately before 1914 there are signs in the new capital creation statistics (Simon, Chapter 1 below) of a revived interest in British lending to Europe. Aspects of the diplomacy of intra-European capital flows before 1914 have been explored in Feis' *Europe, the World's Banker 1870–1914*, but little attention has been given as yet to the purely market elements in this process other than in terms of short-term international capital movements.

Not only is the debate being reported here incomplete in the senses just indicated it is also incomplete because it has concentrated on an examination of the broad aggregates land, labour, and capital and on a highly simplified apparatus for investigating these interrelationships. In these days, when it is the fashion among economists to experiment with models of this simple character and when it is becoming the fashion for economic historians to rush in and 'test' these simple models with the aid of more or less sophisticated statistical procedures, it is probably salutory that a plea should be made for greater recognition of the historical importance of types of processes and events which do not fit easily into these analytical systems.

This point may be well illustrated by one particular class of event – the discovery of particular mineral resources – though it is, of course, not limited to events of this type. If one takes a sufficiently broad view of the process of British (and other European) capital exports then the sequence of discoveries of major mineral deposits may be interpreted as implicit in the generalized concept of investment in land and of no special analytical significance. At the right level of generality of the argument this is perfectly legitimate and, indeed, essential for the process of analysis. If, on the other hand, one is concerned with the history of a particular country at a particular point of time, then the finding of a particular mineral (in one year rather than another, at one point in a process of fluctuation rather than another, with its own peculiarities of transformation from an ore into a refined mineral and in a particular location) will significantly affect the detailed response of that economy and intimately shape its subsequent development. To mention just one or two notable examples, the exact location and timing of the discovery of diamonds and gold in South Africa and of gold and silver in Australia were at least as important for the particular historical sequence of events in those countries as was the generalized process of the movement of the factors labour and capital. Unless the uniqueness of historical events is kept well to the fore economic history can easily degenerate into something which is neither economics nor history.

The preceding discussion is intended to provide the context for the particular studies that follow. The way in which Williamson's, Ford's, and Habakkuk's articles fit into the debate has already been briefly indicated. Thomas's article is a valuable short statement of the crux of the probable inter-connections between the international flows of labour and capital in the pre-1914 world economy. The editor's contri-bution is a brief attempt to formulate part of the economic mechanism whereby capital flows were linked with building booms in the borrowing countries. This analysis was developed with particular reference to Australian experience in the 1880s. Readers may judge for themselves how relevant it is to Canada's major episode of oversea borrowing in the decade or so before 1914 which is examined by Cairncross.

The remaining article, that by Simon, requires slightly more extended comment. Its function is to provide part of the essential background that is necessary for any examination of pre-1914 British capital exports. Regarded as a first approximation, it does this very well. At the same time readers unfamiliar with his data need to be warned of some of their limitations. As Simon clearly points out, the statistics which he presents are gross figures for new money called up through the British capital market. While this was the major formal mechanism through which British capital flowed it was not the only one. Purchases and sales, some of which were never listed in London, were made of securities on the Stock Exchanges of Paris, Berlin, New York, Johannesburg, Melbourne, etc. Deposits were raised in Britain on a large scale by banks operating abroad. While nominally short term, their accumulation over a period of years could have the same economic effects as a long-term capital flow. Direct investment by individuals or partnerships and increasingly by companies is not included. Redemptions, while relatively unimportant in total, could on occasion be significant for particular countries at particular times. The combined effect of all these omissions is that the new creation statistics, valuable as they are as a guide to the scale and complexity of British oversea investment before 1914, are not an accurate measure of the volume, timing, and amplitude of the fluctuations in British capital exports.

1 The Pattern of New British Portfolio Foreign Investment, 1865–1914

MATTHEW SIMON

[This article was first published in J. H. Adler (ed.) *Capital Movements and Economic Development*, Macmillan, 1967.]

'If in the next half century we are to create £5,000 or £6,000 millions more, what is to be the issue?'[1]

Viewed from the vantage point of 1965 the international capital movements of the first half of the preceding century (1865–1914) exercised a unique, profound, and long-run impact on the structure and the development of the world economy. The political and social repercussions of the pre-1914 foreign investments have, in turn, been a decisive factor in the world politics of the past five decades. As the leading creditor nation in the pre-1914 era, British international capital movements played a prominent and commanding role in these processes. At the very climax of this era, in 1914, C. K. Hobson initiated a systematic inquiry into the causes and effects of British foreign investment. To increase our understanding of this complex phenomenon he recognized the necessity to examine the reciprocal interplay between economic and political forces, apply the tools of economic analysis, and construct estimates of international capital movements and their components.

This paper, as the second phase of an investigation of the global aspects of international capital movements, presents a new comprehensive set of annual series of new British portfolio foreign investment for the half century ending in 1914.[2]

---

[1] Robert Louis Nash, *Fenn's Compendium of The English Foreign Funds* (London: Effingham Wilson, Royal Exchange, 9th Edition, 1867), p. xi.

[2] Harvey Segal and Matthew Simon, 'British Foreign Capital Issues, 1865–94', *Journal of Economic History*, December 1961, pp. 567–81.

Following in Hobson's tradition of analysing cause and effect, we recognize the need to identify as accurately as possible the pattern of British capital exports. To learn more precisely who did the borrowing, in what form, and for what purposes, and in what amounts will serve this end.

The first part of the paper explains the nature and the development of the new statistics against the background of previous efforts of estimating the capital account of the British balance of payments. This is followed by an overall survey of what the new figures show for the entire fifty years. The third section identifies major trends and fluctuations in the pattern of pre-1914 British foreign investment. In the concluding section we compare the new data with related statistics and suggest some of the implications for further research and analysis.

I

The development of the quantitative record of pre-1914 British international capital movements has had a long history. The literature contains three types of statistical data: annual estimates of net international capital movements and of new overseas issues and estimates of the value of aggregate British holdings (and components thereof), of foreign and colonial securities for particular years.

These data are not mutually exclusive. Several writers, including Brinley Thomas in his comprehensive and provocative paper prepared for this Conference, have indicated and stressed the complementary nature of these statistics by employing them to validate the accuracy of particular estimates.[1] In addition, other students, notably A. G. Ford,[2] have utilized

---

[1] Brinley Thomas, 'The Historical Record of International Capital Movements to 1913' (Paper for International Economic Association Conference on Capital Movements and Economic Development, Washington, July 1965), pp. 1–7.

[2] A. G. Ford, 'The Transfer of British Foreign Lending 1870–1913', *Economic History Review*, December 1958, pp. 302–8; *The Gold Standard 1880–1914 Britain and Argentina* (Oxford: Clarendon Press, 1962), chap. iv, esp. pp. 52–7, 62–70; 'Bank Rate, The British Balance of Payments and the Burden of Adjustment, 1870–1914', *Oxford Economic Papers*, March 1964, pp. 24–39.

these statistics to provide an empirical basis for specific models they have constructed to explain the course of British foreign investment before 1914. It is, therefore, necessary to examine the characteristics and uses of each of these three types of statistics.

Annual estimates of the net international capital movements of Great Britain, calculated as the residuals of the balance of payments accounts, have been prepared for all or most of the half century before 1914 by Hobson, Cairncross, and Imlah.[1] Although subject to various margins of error arising largely from the assumptions made in estimating current account invisible items, these figures serve two purposes. First, they facilitate the study of secular and cyclical changes in the relative importance of aggregate net foreign investment in the British economy and in the relationships between net international capital movements and various parts of the current account of the British balance of payments. Moreover, they provide benchmarks for the fruitful examination of independently derived estimates of individual components of the capital account.

Various contemporaries have employed a second method of estimating the value of the aggregate portfolio of foreign and colonial securities of British investors – with regional and industrial breakdowns – at particular points during the fifty-year span. George Paish, editor of *The Statist*, developed a set of such 'stock' estimates for 1907 by capitalizing the yield from outstanding investments at an appropriate rate. He then used annual new issues to obtain similar figures for the end of 1913.[2] These statistics, to be sure, suffer from incompleteness of

[1] C. K. Hobson, *The Export of Capital* (New York: The Macmillan Company, 1914) chap. vii; A. K. Cairncross, *Home and Foreign Investment, 1870–1913* (Cambridge: Cambridge University Press, 1958), chap. vi; A. H. Imlah, *Economic Elements in the Pax Britannica* (Cambridge: Harvard University Press, 1958), chap. iii.

[2] Sir George Paish, 'Great Britain's Investments in Other Lands', *Journal of The Royal Statistical Society*, lxxi (September 1909), 456–80; 'Great Britain's Capital Investments in Individual Colonial and Foreign Countries', ibid., lxxxiv (January 1911), 167–200; 'Export of Capital and The Cost of Living', *The Statist*, lxxix (February 1914), Supplement; Herbert Feis, *Europe The World's Banker 1870–1914* (New Haven: Yale University Press, 1930), pp. 17–32. Feis revised Paish's original estimates.

coverage. Moreover, they reflect secular, cyclical, and random fluctuations in the market prices of the outstanding holdings of British investors. The latter changes clearly are not a product of capital account transactions of the balance of international payments. The stock statistics, nevertheless, provide a guide to the geographic distribution and industrial composition of British foreign investment.[1]

The third procedure has been the direct method of estimating individual components of the capital account. It has been impossible to develop annual measures of short-term capital movements or of long-term direct overseas investments.[2] Greater success has been obtained with statistics of portfolio foreign investment, which occupied a pre-eminent position in pre-1914 British long-term capital movements. Portfolio foreign investment can, in turn, be decomposed into total British purchases of new overseas issues, international movements in outstanding securities and redemptions of such British-held securities by foreign and colonial nations.[3]

Research has concentrated on the development and use of overseas new issue statistics. In his pioneering investigation of British foreign investment Leland H. Jenks developed estimates of new foreign capital issues.[4] *The Investor's Monthly Manual*, a supplement of The London *Economist*, has been regarded as the principal source of pre-1914 new issue statistics. Beginning in February 1865, this periodical regularly published monthly tables containing lists of publicly offered new securities, together with the amounts 'created' and 'called'. In their

[1] For other sets of stock estimates see Cairncross, *Home and Foreign Investment*, pp. 183, 185, and A. R. Hall, *The London Capital Market and Australia 1870–1914* (Canberra: The Australian National University Press, 1963), pp. 9, 11, 13, 90, 161.

[2] Arthur I. Bloomfield, *Short-Term Capital Movements Under the Pre-1914 Gold Standard* (Princeton, New Jersey: International Finance Section, Department of Economics, Princeton University 1963), pp. 49–50.

[3] Conceptually, net portfolio foreign investment is equal to total overseas issues – redemptions of outstanding issues – movements in outstanding securities. We neglect in this formulation as insignificant both British new issues floated in overseas markets and redemptions of outstanding British securities in the pre-1914 era.

[4] Leland H. Jenks, *The Migration of British Capital to 1875* (New York: Alfred A. Knopf, 1927), pp. 419–26.

terms a capital creation 'includes only that part of the registered capital offered for immediate subscription by the public'. And excluded, where ascertainable, vendors' shares.[1] In listing specific creations, *The Investor's Monthly Manual* did not practise consistency. It would often record the gross total of the nominal amount offered, and on other occasions the actual market price at which the issue was disposed.

C. K. Hobson used *The Investor's Monthly Manual* creations data to develop annual estimates of new overseas issues offered in the British capital market between 1870 and 1913. He included both those issues floated exclusively in Great Britain ('the all-British issues') as well as those floated simultaneously in Great Britain and other places ('the partials'). Hobson assumed that one-half of the latter category in the aggregate was offered in Great Britain and added that amount to the 'all-British' component to obtain his series.[2]

The use of *The Investor's Monthly Manual* creation statistics as a measure of new British portfolio foreign investment and as an indicator of the net export of capital has been challenged on a variety of grounds. First, the amount offered for subscription may not be absorbed by the investing public. The issue may thus be totally or partially withdrawn by the responsible financial institution. The vendors also may have second thoughts and take a portion of the issue. Moreover, even if the entire issue is sold the amount of funds actually called from investors may represent only a fraction of the total.[3]

In 1961, Harvey Segal and I presented a paper that was designed in part to offset the limitations of the creation statistics. We realized the need for and the significance of accurate information on the money calls, the actual payments made

[1] *The Investor's Monthly Manual*, December 1865, 374.

[2] C. K. Hobson, *The Export of Capital*, p. 219. It is misleading to suggest, as does Cairncross, that Hobson used money calls in his analysis of British foreign investment. Cf. A. K. Cairncross, 'The English Capital Market Before 1914', *Economica*, May 1958, p. 142.

[3] See the excellent discussions in C. K. Hobson, *The Export of Capital*, 209–11; N. G. Butlin, *Australian Domestic Product, Investment and Foreign Borrowing, 1861–1938/39* (Cambridge, at The University Press, 1962), pp. 405–6; A. R. Hall, 'The English Capital Market Before 1914 – A Reply', *Economica*, November 1958, 342; and *The London Capital Market*, pp. 87–8, 203–6.

by British investors in acquiring foreign and colonial issues. In a more fundamental sense it was necessary to examine each issue and the associated transactions in creation and calls in order to construct a complete universe of new overseas lending.

By focusing on the individual issue as the point of departure in the investigation, we could compile and develop valuable information on the geographic, political, and economic characteristics of British overseas lending. To achieve this objective we established an elaborate numerical code that facilitated the classification of each issue by the following attributes of the borrower: (A) continent and country; (B) political status; (C) climatic-ethnic region; (D) type of issuer; (E) industry of issuer; and (F) the kind of security issued. The code contains almost one hundred and eighty countries on seven continents, ninety industrial groups that have been consolidated into ten sectors and various combinations, and extensive subdivisions of the type of issuer and other classifications. With the assistance of contemporary sources such as the *Stock Exchange Year Book* and Burdett's *Stock Exchange Official Intelligence*, we proceeded to identify and code more than 9,100 foreign and colonial transactions from *The Investor's Monthly Manual's* monthly listings of creations and calls for the period 1865–94. The data on each transaction was then punched on a card. The information on all the cards was placed on magnetic tape, and with the aid of a carefully prepared and elaborate programme, an IBM 704 computer generated a vast output of monthly and annual time series and matrices or cross-tabulations in less than an hour.[1] The paper we prepared summarized the salient features of the basic data which provided new insights into the geographic distribution and industrial composition of new British foreign investment. It also illustrated the possibilities and fruitfulness of data-processing techniques in illuminating the quantitative aspects of international capital movements.

The present paper employs the same basic procedure for the

[1] At this point, I would like to acknowledge the innovating role of Harvey Segal in conceiving the 'grand design' of constructing an elaborate code and of employing the electronic computer to cope with this problem.

entire period 1865–1914. It, however, introduces several important innovations with the result that the new figures presented here are not comparable with the statistics contained in the 1961 paper. First, the earlier study confined its compilation to *The Investor's Monthly Manual* monthly lists, with a minimum of corrections. Subsequent research indicated that this source contained a variety of errors and omissions. Calls were not reported completely for many issues. In many instances, especially for small or private ventures, only the nominal initial payments accompanying the application for the issue were recorded. In other cases, particularly for government and railroad issues, the substantial payments made when the securities were allotted to the investor were omitted.[1] Besides, *The Investor's Monthly Manual* excluded private placements, omitted some offerings in the provinces and in foreign capital markets and even missed selected publicly offered issues in London throughout the entire period. In short, it was necessary to rely on a wide variety of sources that included Burdett's *Stock Exchange Official Intelligence*, *The Stock Exchange Yearbook*, *The Parliamentary Papers*, various financial journals, and above all, a vast mass of unpublished research material on British foreign capital issues that was provided by Leland Jenks ('The Jenks Files')[2] to compensate for the above deficiencies. We were then able to construct more complete creation and call estimates of new British portfolio foreign investments that included data on publicly offered issues on London, the Provinces, and non-British capital markets and private placements.

Second, in our first presentation, we followed the procedure of *The Investor's Monthly Manual* and differentiated between the 'all British' and 'partial' issues. Although series were compiled for both, our analysis of the data was confined to the former sector. In this paper, we eliminated the artificial distinction

---

[1] This consistent bias towards under-reporting calls was corrected by analysis of the monthly lists of calls of *The Inventor's Monthly Manual*, which contained a column, 'already paid' that provided the basis for the correcting adjustment.

[2] The Jenks files refer to a massive parallel investigation that was conducted in England before 1940. It relied on the available abundant material in London and focused on assembling annual data on net capital subscribed.

between the two types of issues by estimating the British share of the partials to obtain more complete statistics of total new British portfolio foreign investment. This objective was accomplished by rejecting C. K. Hobson's technique of assuming that the British component of the annual aggregate partial security flotations constituted 50 per cent of the total in favour of a thorough examination of each issue to determine as precisely as possible the amount of British capital subscribed.[1]

The final innovation involved the more systematic treatment of conversions. In our original presentation, the statistics derived from *The Investor's Monthly Manual* compilations included some conversion issues. Conceptually, it is necessary to distinguish between two types of conversions: 'swap conversions' and 'export conversions'. A 'swap conversion' involved the exchange of a new issue for an old issue that was entirely in the hands of British investors. A variant would be the sale of a new flotation to a particular group of British investors to retire obligations possessed by another group of British security holders. In both cases, no new British long-term capital was forthcoming. 'Export conversions', on the other hand, required the sale of new issues to British investors to retire floating or short-term debt held either in Great Britain, the borrowing nation or third countries, or long-term debt that was held in either the borrowing nation or in third countries. In each instance, new long-term British capital would be mobilized for foreign investment.[2] It is therefore necessary to include the 'export conversions' as part of new British portfolio foreign investment. The Type of Issuer segment of the code was, consequently, modified to reflect this distinction and to facilitate the proper classification of each transaction.

[1] Commenting on C. K. Hobson's 50 per cent assumption, A. R. Hall states: 'This assumption appears to be generous for 1895–1899. It may lead to some understatement of total overseas issues in the last decade of the series.' A. R. Hall, 'A Note on The English Capital Market Before 1914', *Economica*, February 1957, p. 62.

[2] C. K. Hobson, *The Export of Capital*, p. 211. It should be noted that the flotation of security in Great Britain by a foreign borrower to retire short-term obligations held in Great Britain signifies that the United Kingdom is exporting long-term capital and importing short-term capital.

The accomplishment of these three major operations for the entire period 1865–1914 required the accurate coding of more than 41,000 separate transactions (including more than 1,000 'swap conversions') and the punching of an equivalent number of cards. With a revised and more elaborate programme to provide additional matrices, an IBM 7094 computer in June 1965 – as a mark of technical progress – completed the operations in less than a hour!

II

We will first present the data on money calls in the form of fifty-year totals to obtain an overall view of the experience of the entire half century. Aggregate new British portfolio foreign

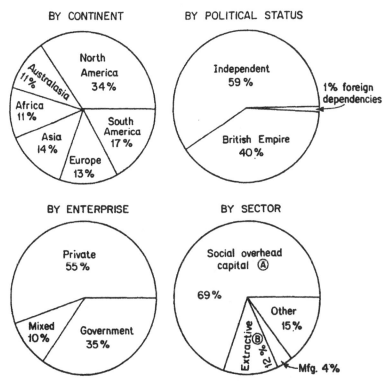

Ⓐ Includes transportation, public utilities and public works

Ⓑ Includes agriculture and mining

CHART I

investment approximated £4,082,000,000 and occupied a pre-eminent position in total British capital exports.[1]

Chart 1 provides a breakdown of this total by four major classifications: continent, political status, industry, and type of enterprise of the issuer. A study of the pattern of pre-1914 British foreign investments shows a dual tendency towards concentration and proliferation. The latter feature, reflecting its almost cosmopolitan character and widespread involvement in diverse enterprises and industries, was especially evident in the last five years (1909–13) before the outbreak of the general war. In that short interval, almost 24 per cent of the total British capital called for the five decades was mobilized for overseas borrowers.

An examination of the chart presenting the continental breakdown shows that the New World received more than 51 per cent, or almost £2,100 million, of the total. North America, the leading continent, absorbed almost £1,400 million and far outstripped the other areas. Nevertheless, each of the remaining continents, illustrating the proliferation process, received at least 10 per cent of new British long-term capital exports.

If the political status criterion is employed, we find that approximately 60 per cent of new British overseas lending went to independent countries and slightly less than 40 per cent to the Empire. The availability of abundant private ventures with attractive prospects for remuneration and appreciation and the expanding needs of various public authorities, especially in the independent countries of the New World and to a lesser degree in Europe and Asia, more than counterbalanced the real or 'alleged' advantages associated with the protection of the British flag.[2]

---

[1] If we subtract the 1914 figure of £203·0 million, the forty-nine-year total is £3,879·0 million, which can be compared, subject to the qualifications stated in the previous section, with Feis' adjustment of the Paish stock estimate of £4,014 million.

[2] It should be noted that this 60 per cent–40 per cent division of new British foreign portfolio investment compares favourably with Paish's 52 per cent–48 per cent split of total British foreign security holdings. This disparity can, in part, be explained by the growing capacity of the independent developed nations of North America and of Europe to repurchase their own securities and to acquire foreign issues from the British.

A fruitful method to study the composition of long-term capital exports is to determine its division among the major climatic-ethnic categories.

The great bulk of trans-European British investment – approximately 68 per cent, or £2,400 million – flowed to the temperate regions of recent settlement. Only 27 per cent, or less than £960 million, was absorbed by the tropics, and the remaining 5 per cent, or slightly over £180 million, was received by non-tropical Asia. The greatest capital-exporting nation of the pre-1914 world was thus supplying an annual average of less than £20 million in new funds to those densely populated tropical regions which, by 1965 standards, are regarded as the most underdeveloped areas of the world.[1] The tropical section of the British Empire, including India, Egypt, and Malaysia, received a total of £510 million, or slightly more than £10 million a year.

The Type of Issuers classification shows a diverse mix of enterprises obtaining new long-term funds in the British capital market. Private firms, with almost 55 per cent of the total, occupied the primary position. Colonial and foreign governmental bodies – national, provincial and local – received 35 per cent of the aggregate money calls for both additional requirements and export conversions. Mixed enterprises, distinguished by the contractual arrangements which they concluded with various public authorities providing for the guarantee of interest payments on their obligations, absorbed the remaining 10 per cent.

A study of the Economic Sector breakdown impressively demonstrates the significance of overseas lending for the purpose of building the social overhead capital of the borrowing nations. This category, which includes transportation, public utilities, and other public works, received almost 70 per cent of new British foreign portfolio investment. Transportation, the largest industrial segment, obtained at least 46 per cent, and railroads, its major component, 41 per cent of the

[1] Ragnar Nurkse, 'The Problem of International Investment Today in The Light of Nineteenth-Century Experience', *Economic Journal*, lxiv (December 1954), p. 750.

total.[1] By contrast, less than 12 per cent was invested in the extractive industries. The emphasis was thus placed on the development of those facilities which increased the capacity of primary producing nations to export marketable surpluses to Europe. Finally, it is abundantly clear that British funds did not directly foster the development of extensive overseas industrialization as less than 4 per cent of the total capital called was invested in manufacturing.

The use of our classification system provides some interesting insights into the industrial and regional concentration and spread of British foreign investment. Alan Hall attributes its geographical proliferation to the flexibility of British investors, who shifted their horizons in the wake of the appearance of new opportunities. He writes: 'This unevenness in the rate of lending to particular areas meant that the greater part of the investment outstanding in 1914 had occurred in relatively short periods of time. This certainly was the case with Australia and there is plenty of evidence that her experience was not exceptional.'[2]

Our data supports his contention strongly for Australasia, Southeast Asia, and possibly South Africa, areas in which one large spurt provided a significant portion of the total capital invested. It has substantial validity for Russia, Canada, and Latin America. Hall's notion, however, is not relevant to the United States, which experienced an almost continuous influx of foreign capital, punctuated by sharp reversals in the late 1870s and the 1890s. In fact, it seems legitimate to infer from the data showing the fifty-year pattern contained in Chart 1, that the single most important force accounting for the primacy of North America among the continents, independent countries in the Political Status categories, the regions of recent settlements among the climatic-ethnic groups, private enterprise in the type of issuers, and finally, social overhead capital among

---

[1] We say 'at least' because it is difficult to determine precisely these amounts owing to the variegated character of government expenditures on public works. In addition it is likely that the 'miscellaneous' classification, consisting of almost 3 per cent of the total and represented almost exclusively by governmental bodies, contains some outlays for transportation and railways.

[2] A. R. Hall, *The London Capital Market*, p. 189.

the economic sectors, was the huge demands for building and maintaining the 216,000 miles of the American rail net, constructed largely under private auspices in this epoch. Nor was it an accident that the largest department of the London Stock Exchange was American Railroads and the subtitle of Burdett's *Stock Exchange Official Intelligence* was 'A Precis of English, *American* and Foreign Securities'. Aggregate new British long-term portfolio investment in the United States, surpassing the amount placed in all of Latin America, exceeded £835 million and constituted almost 21 per cent of the total.

This phenomenon might appear paradoxical in view of the successful maturation of the American economy, which provided the basis of the rapid accumulation of capital throughout this period. Modern experience has shown that the largest volume of international trade takes place between developed or rapidly developing economies. The same point may be made for international capital movements. Just as post-1919 United States has had a low propensity to import but has remained the largest single importer in international trade due to its high level of economic activity, so the United States of 1865–1914, with a declining propensity to finance her total investment requirements by overseas borrowing, was the single most important foreign source of new security issues in the British capital market.[1]

In short, a nation, experiencing the largest absolute increments in national output and capital formation, may play a formidable role in foreign capital markets. The concentration and proliferation aspects of new British foreign portfolio investment was thus manifest in a spectrum extending from rapidly developing countries, especially the United States, to the tropics, colonial and non-colonial.

---

[1] S. B. Saul, *Studies in British Overseas Trade* (Liverpool: Liverpool University Press, 1960), p. 66. Foreign holdings of American securities on 30 June 1914, aggregated $5,400,000,000. See United States Department of Commerce, *Historical Statistics of The United States, Colonial Times to 1957* (Washington, D.C.: Superintendent of Documents, U.S. Government Printing Office, 1960), p. 565; Matthew Simon, 'The United States Balance of Payments, 1861–1900', *Trends In the American Economy in The Nineteenth Century*, Studies in Income and Wealth, xxiv, pp. 629–711.

III

Our basic annual time series for total British portfolio foreign investment in money calls appear in Charts 2 through 4 and the Appendix Table. They provide the basis for the following discussion of trends and fluctuations.

In Chart 2, where the data on aggregate capital called for the entire world and particular continents have been plotted, we find no evidence of a persisted trend extending over the five decades. Each series (even North America) is subject to major reversals in direction, that reflect both changes in the volume of aggregate new British foreign portfolio investment and its periodic geographic redistribution.

Nor, despite the importance attached by some writers to the Empire, do we find evidence of a trend to invest in that area, at the expense of independent countries.[1] Others, notably John Hobson and various Marxists, have argued that the pressure to export capital arising within a developed capitalist economy in the United Kingdom was the principal force generating the overseas expansion of the British Empire, which, in turn led to a redirection of capital towards newly acquired territories.[2] An examination of the first three panels in Chart 3 shows that, although substantial absolute increases in the amount of new British foreign portfolio investment occurred in both independent countries and the Empire, the Empire portion displays no persistent trend. Those writers who emphasize the shift from Europe to the Empire neglect the significance of pre-1870 investments in Indian government and railroad securities and over-estimate the importance of the pattern prevailing in the hectic pre-1873 prosperous years and during the aftermath of the Franco-Prussian war. After reaching a peak in 1885 of 67

[1] For example, 'but from the mid-1870s onwards investment in Empire became more and more important', S. B. Saul, *Studies*, p. 67, and 'the long-term trend after 1873 was away from Europe to the primary producing countries and *especially* toward those within the Empire', A. R. Hall, *The London Capital Market*, p. 12.

[2] For a recent discussion, see D. K. Fieldhouse, 'Imperialism: An Historiographical Revision', *The Economic History Review*, xiv, no. 2, December 1961, pp. 187–209.

per cent following a surge of investment in Australasia, the Empire share declines to 25 per cent in 1890. It rises during the mining boom in Australia in the 1890s and advances to a

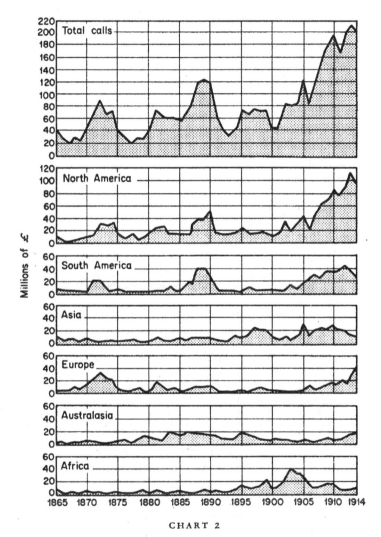

CHART 2

high of 59 per cent in 1903, following the termination of the Boer War. From that time, the Empire portion declines to a level somewhat below 40 per cent in the last three pre-war years.

With the exception of South Africa, most of the territory

acquired by the British Empire in this period was located in the tropics. An examination of the last panel of Chart 3 indicates the absence of any tendency to invest an increasing share in the tropics, which included India, an area acquired before 1800.

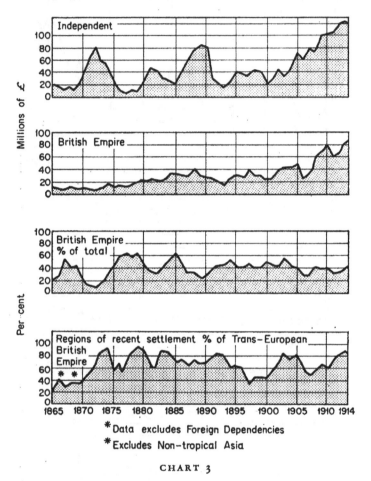

CHART 3

On the contrary, the great mass of British capital exported to the overseas Empire gravitated towards the regions of recent settlement. In the case of South Africa, new British portfolio foreign investment evolved through four stages: Advancing sharply from £1·5 million to £12·8 million in 1899, collapsing to an annual level of £2·4 million during the years of the Boer War (1900–1), reaching a new peak of £36·1 million in the immediate post-war aftermath in 1903, and declining to under £5 million in the last three pre-war years. These statistics cast serious doubt about the crucial importance of the 'New Empire' as an outlet for British capital exports.

In the pre-1914 pattern, private enterprises acquired an increased importance among foreign and colonial flotations in the British capital market. Evidence of this trend can be found

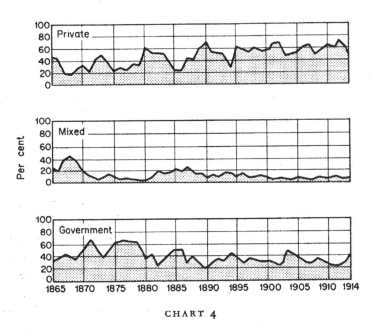

CHART 4

in Chart 4, where the data by type of issuer by shares of total calls is plotted.

The decline in the portion absorbed by mixed enterprises is attributable to two sets of factors, geographic shifts and the process of general development. Prior to 1875, British investors bought substantial quantities of the issues of the state guaranteed railroads of India and Russia. The relative importance of these borrowers declined after that date. Of greater significance was the growth of such underdeveloped areas as Latin America Canada, and other parts of the Empire. This condition produced the revision of contractual arrangements between governments and railroads completed or in the process of contraction. Interest guarantee provisions were frequently eliminated. In other cases, new railroads and other public facilities were established without such support from government agencies. More fundamentally, the rapid, although uneven development of these areas and the United States – reflected in rising population, increased urbanization and the expansion of the markets for their primary products – opened up vast opportunities for private enterprise in the social overhead, extractive, and real estate sectors. As a result, although the absolute volume of government borrowing advanced, substantially, its relative position among issuers declined and that of private borrowers rose substantially.

An examination of Charts 2–4 and the Appendix Table indicates that new long-term British capital exports were characterized by a complex set of fluctuations including long swings, shorter cyclical movements and shifts arising from wars and changing international relations. The ensuing discussion will focus on the long swings.

Over the fifty-year span we find almost two-and-one-half long swings in the aggregate series on total capital called for the entire world. It is realistic to assume that the first long swing commenced in 1862 and following the sharp reversal after the Overend Gurney panic of 1866, reaches a peak in 1872, one year before the beginning of the world-wide cyclical depression.[1] The contraction phase of the first long swing culminates in 1877, two years before the onset of the revival of general business activity. The expansion phase of the second long swing extends to a peak in 1889, which precedes the Baring Panic of the following year. The ensuing decline is especially pronounced in the early 1890s and reaches a bottom in 1893. Owing to the anaemic character of the recovery in the 1890s and the adverse impact of the Boer War on new overseas lending we place the trough of the second long swing in

---

[1] The 1862 date is based on Imlah's data on net international capital movements. See Albert H. Imlah, *Economic Elements in the Pax Britannica* (Cambridge, Massachusetts: Harvard University, 1958) pp. 72–5, and the table and discussion, in Jeffrey Williamson, *American Growth and The Balance of Payments 1820–1913* (Chapel Hill: The University of North Carolina Press, 1964), pp. 208–10.

1901.[1] The upswing of the next long cycle then proceeds vigorously to reach a peak, one year before the outbreak of the First World War.

In Table I, we have assembled the dates of the troughs and peaks of the long swings and the levels prevailing in those years for the major components of the principal classifications of the data. Observe the clustering of the turning points of various series around 1872, 1877, 1889, 1901, and 1913. An analysis of the data will show that the intensity of the swings, as reflected in per cent changes between peaks and troughs, for the following series – Independent Countries, Regions of Recent Settlement, North America, South America, Europe, the United States, Private Enterprise, Manufacturing, Railroads and Social Overhead Capital – are generally greater or almost equal to the comparable changes in the world total. By contrast, with the exception of the third long cycle, less pronounced swings can be found in the British Empire, Mixed Enterprise, and Government Series. Moreover, little evidence can be found of the two-and-half cycle sequence in the Australian, African, and Asian series. Africa experiences no major upswing prior to 1875, rises sharply between 1893 and 1903 – due to the mining boom and the aftermath of the Boer War – and trends downward to the war. Australia's behaviour is similarly perverse as it rises in the mid-1870s due to government borrowing for railroads and public works and peaks in 1886. In the mid-1890s it rises again due to the West Australian gold-mining boom and then declines in the early twentieth century until the immediate pre-war years.[2] Similarly, Asia shows no surge in the early 1870s, but does participate in the upswings of the second and third cycles.

The fluctuations in the volume of capital called for total new British portfolio foreign investment is largely, though not entirely, ascribable to the sharp fluctuations in the North American, the United States, Independent Nations, and

[1] Ibid. Using Douglas's data, Brinley Thomas asserts: 'The years 1888 to 1901-2 saw a downswing in foreign lending' cf. Brinley Thomas, *Migration and Economic Growth* (Cambridge: at the University Press, 1954), p. 98.
[2] Alan R. Hall, *The London Capital Market*, pp. 189-91.

TABLE I *Long-swing Dating and Levels for Turning Points in New British Portfolio Foreign Investment and Major Components, 1865–1914*

(Millions of £ in Money Calls)

Series	First peak	First trough	Second peak	Second trough	Third peak
World total	93·9	19·4	122·9	49·5	217·4
	1872	1877	1889	1901	1913
Political status					
Independent countries	84·4	6·6	87·4	20·2	126·9
	1872	1877	1889	1900	1913
British Empire	20·9	13·3	42·2	24·0	90·9
	1874	1877	1888	1901	1914
Climatic-ethnic					
Regions of recent settlement	40·9	8·5	86·4	24·7	148·0
	1874	1877	1890	1900	1913
Tropics	22·7	4·7	27·9	12·1	68·7
	1872	1879	1888	1901	1910
Continents and country					
North America	33·1	4·3	52·8	10·7	116·9
	1874	1877	1890	1900	1913
South America	21·4	0·6	40·2	4·5	45·8
	1871	1877	1889	1902	1912
Europe	34·8	3·7	12·3	0·8	43·5
	1872	1877	1890	1904	1914
United States	25·4	1·6	44·8	5·5	53·9
	1872	1877	1890	1900	1913
Enterprise					
Private	41·4	4·4	86·6	29·3	152·4
	1872	1877	1890	1900	1912
Mixed		7·7	23·3	1·7	17·1
		1876	1887	1903	1914
Government	41·9	13·2	53·5	14·0	95·5
	1871	1877	1888	1901	1914
Industry and sector					
Manufacturing	1·1	—	18·2	1·2	21·1
	1872	1879	1890	1900	1912
Railroad	34·2	7·1	57·6	14·9	88·6
	1872	1877	1890	1900	1913
Social overhead capital	66·2	15·2	89·8	31·9	176·4
	1872	1877	1888	1900	1914
Extractive	7·0	0·5	14·2	9·9	51·8
	1872	1879	1889	1900	1910

Regions of Recent Settlements Series.[1] In each of these areas, private enterprise played the principal and increasingly significant role. The flow of funds in the form of money calls to these private issuers was moulded by two sets of influences. The demand of foreign borrowers for new British capital was first determined by their changing appraisals of their profit prospects. The second force was the ability and willingness of the British investors to lend. Their actions were principally affected by their appraisal of profit prospects, including the risk factor in the borrowing nation, the state of the British money market, and alternative opportunities in Great Britain and other foreign areas.

To contend, then, that the long swings in aggregate new British foreign investments were induced by the long swings in the capital called by the United States and other areas in the regions of recent settlements is to suggest the existence and persistence of a significant differential or the widening of the differential in bond yields and profit prospects, in favour of the borrowing nation over the expansion phase of the long cycle. The reverse condition, reflected in the diminution of capital called, would prevail in the contraction phase of the long swing.

These observations are preliminary and partial. They point up the statistical evidence for long swings in our data but do not attempt to provide a logical basis for their periodicity. Moreover, they omit an appraisal of the significant role of foreign public borrowing in affecting fluctuations in aggregate new overseas lending. An inspection of the data in the Appendix Table and Chart 4 shows that the volume of capital called by foreign and colonial government displayed less volatility than private borrowing. In shorter cyclical contractions, the government share tended to rise and, on some occasions, notably 1907–8, the absolute magnitudes of calls experienced a substantial increase. On balance, the movements in aggregate volume of government borrowing conformed with the long swings in total new portfolio foreign investments. Further study of the data in disaggregated form may shed additional light on this problem.

[1] See comparable discussion in Jeffrey Williamson ,*American Growth* ,pp. 212–16.

IV

In this final section the basic aggregate series are compared with related statistics. In Table II (columns 1 and 4) we observe that Imlah's series on net international capital movements shows a close correspondence with the money calls series on total new British portfolio foreign investment. In both series are found the big surges of the early 1870s, the late 1880s, and the decade 1904–13, and the depressed periods of the 1870s and the 1890s. Imlah's long swing turning points are 1872, 1877, 1890, 1898, and 1913. Whereas the corresponding peaks and troughs for portfolio foreign investment calls are 1872, 1877, 1889, 1901, and 1913. The two series moved together in 32 out of the 48 years, or 66·7 per cent of the time. The lack of greater congruence is not surprising since variations in new portfolio foreign investment may be offset in many years by movements in outstanding securities, redemptions, and the short-term capital account.

A comparison of Hobson's creation statistics with our creation series (columns 2 and 3 of Table II) shows they move together in 37 out of 40 years. It will be observed that Hobson's figures for 1871 and 1872 are substantially greater because his 50 per cent assumption for the partials is too high for the French war and indemnity loans. In most of the remaining years, our statistics are somewhat larger than Hobson's primarily due to the omissions of *The Investor's Monthly Manual* upon which his series is based. To a lesser degree, the 50 per cent assumption for partials actually leads to an underestimation of the portion of these issues absorbed by the British in the pre-1914 years.

Our call series can also be compared with the annual new issues data compiled in the Belgian financial periodical, *Le Moniteur Des Interêts Matérielles*, which was published by the De Lavelaye family in Brussels. They attempted to keep account of the total amount of new securities that were floated in all capital markets of the world including those of the borrowing nations. Since their coverage was not as complete as ours, we have confined the comparison to the data on aggregate government, railroad, and manufacturing issues. In Table II, columns 5, 6, 7, the data are presented and we have computed ratios which measure the share of new world capital issues in these sectors represented by new British portfolio foreign investment, for the period 1871–1912. It should be clear from inspecting column 7 that the British share experiences a secular decline. This trend reflects the more rapidly increasing capacity of the capital markets of the United States, France, Germany to absorb new issues.[1]

This introductory paper has concentrated on presenting and describing the basic data in the new series. The fifty-year totals for our major components confirm the extent of the sharply unequal distribution of new British portfolio foreign investment. A relatively small portion was absorbed by the colonial and non-colonial tropics, while the regions of recent settlement – especially independent countries, such as the United States – received more substantial amounts to foster the growth of their social overhead capital. Examination of the annual time series shows the absence of any persistent trend towards particular regions or to the British Empire. Study of the enterprise data demonstrates the increasing importance of private foreign and colonial borrowers as the major source of new security issues in the British capital market. Finally, the statistics for the major series provide support for the existence of approximately two-and-half long swings as a principal form of fluctuation in the half century before 1914.

It now becomes necessary to combine further study with additional research on both general and specific questions in this area. Intensive analysis of the vast body of output of the two-dimensional matrices and of monthly statistics will proceed. Study of the data on redemptions compiled from *The Investor's Monthly Manual* and processed by the same programme on the IBM-7094 will shed additional light on another item in the capital account and add to our understanding of the geographical shifts in pre-1914 British foreign

---

[1] This conclusion could be altered in view of the heavy British absorption of private issues in the transportation sector and public utilities, agriculture, and mining. Unfortunately, the *Moniteur* does not contain such data.

TABLE II *New British Portfolio Foreign Investment and Related Statistics, 1865–1914*

(Millions of £)

	Imlah Net. Int. Cap. Move. (1)	Hobson Creations Total (2)	Brit. New Port. For. Inv. Creations Total (3)	Calls Total (4)	Calls Gov't, (5)	Moniteur Creations RR., Ind. (6)	% 5/6 (7)
1865	34·9	—	59·0	42·5	24·3	—	—
1866	33·0	—	21·6	25·2	17·5	—	—
1867	42·2	—	26·5	18·4	15·5	—	—
1868	36·5	—	37·3	29·1	25·1	—	—
1869	46·7	—	17·8	21·9	16·2	—	—
1870	44·1	45·2	46·2	44·7	32·3	—	—
1871	71·3	84·3	77·5	70·2	60·9	618·6	9·8
1872	98·0	116·8	86·0	93·9	69·2	424·0	16·3
1873	81·3	54·9	79·1	69·3	50·4	363·5	13·9
1874	70·9	64·4	73·7	74·5	61·0	155·5	39·2
1875	51·3	35·2	44·2	46·1	37·0	50·2	73·7
1876	23·2	26·3	28·1	30·4	25·6	141·6	18·1
1877	13·1	13·7	22·9	19·4	16·6	292·8	5·7
1878	16·9	25·0	34·0	31·7	25·0	174·6	14·3
1879	35·5	27·0	34·5	30·5	23·5	278·7	8·4
1880	35·6	40·7	46·3	41·7	28·4	168·2	16·9
1881	65·7	60·0	89·9	74·2	52·5	233·7	22·5
1882	58·7	49·8	78·8	67·5	45·8	164·8	27·8
1883	48·8	45·5	71·9	61·2	55·9	148·5	37·6
1884	72·3	57·0	58·0	63·0	46·5	180·7	25·7
1885	62·3	55·9	52·7	55·3	46·6	124·7	37·4
1886	78·9	56·2	74·4	69·8	56·4	251·7	22·4
1887	87·7	65·8	83·7	84·4	62·6	190·0	32·9
1888	91·9	101·2	133·3	119·1	81·5	295·9	27·5
1889	80·9	107·1	138·5	122·9	74·9	501·9	14·9
1890	98·5	101·3	110·7	116·6	84·4	223·9	37·7
1891	69·4	51·2	51·8	57·6	37·1	225·5	16·5
1892	59·1	32·3	40·1	39·8	25·5	93·5	27·3
1893	53·0	25·2	31·5	32·1	23·3	134·7	17·3
1894	38·7	48·9	43·8	48·3	30·2	191·9	15·7
1895	40·0	57·6	74·2	77·7	34·3	179·5	19·1
1896	56·8	37·3	73·4	68·5	23·7	332·0	7·1
1897	41·6	36·7	77·3	78·4	40·7	318·6	12·8
1898	22·9	51·0	66·6	76·6	51·7	297·3	17·4
1899	42·4	45·9	82·3	78·2	42·8	362·7	11·8
1900	37·9	26·1	50·3	49·6	27·2	415·0	6·6
1901	33·9	27·0	53·7	49·5	34·2	366·6	9·3
1902	33·3	62·2	88·3	89·3	63·1	371·0	18·4
1903	44·8	60·0	82·6	82·9	66·0	326·9	20·2

	Imlah Net. Int. Cap. Move.	Hobson Creations Total	Brit. New Port. For. Inv.			Moniteur	
			Creations Total	Calls Total	Calls Gov't, RR., Ind.	Creations	% 5/6
	(1)	(2)	(3)	(4)	(5)	(6)	(7)
1904	51·7	64·6	87·9	88·0	65·7	446·7	14·7
1905	81·5	110·6	137·0	128·9	98·7	618·3	16·0
1906	117·5	73·0	87·8	85·0	50·2	553·0	9·8
1907	154·1	79·3	110·9	116·3	71·7	599·4	12·0
1908	154·7	117·9	154·7	147·4	110·4	773·9	14·3
1909	135·6	150·5	173·3	175·7	119·1	787·4	15·1
1910	167·3	179·8	203·2	198·0	99·1	801·4	12·4
1911	196·9	142·7	177·8	169·2	101·9	622·8	16·4
1912	197·1	144·6	206·5	200·7	115·6	642·6	18·0
1913	224·3	149·7	206·6	217·4	141·9	—	—
1914	—	—	192·6	203·2	137·2	—	—

(1) Albert M. Imlah, *Economic Elements in the Pax Britannica* (Cambridge, Massachusetts: Harvard University Press 1958), pp. 72–5.

(2) C. K. Hobson, *The Export of Capital* (London: Constable and Co. Ltd., 1914), p. 219.

(3), (4), (5) See discussion in Section I.

(6) Eugene Varga (Editor), *World Economic Crises*, vol. iii, *Monetary Crises* (1821–1938) (Moscow State Financial Press 1939), pp. 832–62. The data was expressed in Belgian francs and was converted at rate of 25·2 francs per £. See Arthur I. Bloomfield, *Short Term Capital Movements Under The Pre-1914 Gold Standard* (Princeton, New Jersey: International Finance Section, Department of Economics, Princeton University, 1963), p. 95.

APPENDIX TABLE *Selected Components of New British Portfolio Foreign Investment (Money Calls), 1865–1914*

(Millions of £)

(I) *By continents**

Year	Europe (1)	North America (2)	South America (3)	Africa (4)	Asia (5)	Australasia (6)	Oceania (7)
1865	7·5	7·1	6·9	8·5	11·2	1·2	0·1
1866	4·5	4·4	4·6	4·1	4·5	3·2	—
1867	4·6	1·5	2·0	0·5	7·5	2·2	—
1868	11·7	3·5	1·5	1·5	8·1	2·8	—
1869	8·0	4·8	0·9	—	6·3	1·9	—
1870	18·6	10·0	4·1	2·2	7·1	2·5	0·3
1871	29·2	13·0	21·4	0·4	3·7	2·5	—

APPENDIX TABLE — (*cont.*)

(I) *By continents**

Year	Europe (1)	North America (2)	South America (3)	Africa (4)	Asia (5)	Australasia (6)	Oceania (7)
1872	34·9	30·8	21·4	1·9	2·2	2·8	—
1873	25·4	26·8	8·0	1·2	4·1	3·8	—
1874	24·7	33·1	5·7	0·5	5·9	4·6	—
1875	10·1	12·2	8·4	4·5	4·0	6·9	—
1876	5·0	9·3	1·5	2·1	5·1	7·4	—
1877	3·7	4·3	0·6	1·7	6·7	2·5	—
1878	6·1	6·2	1·9	3·2	5·0	9·3	—
1879	3·3	7·2	1·1	5·6	0·7	12·4	—
1880	2·7	18·3	3·1	2·7	3·2	11·7	—
1881	20·6	22·2	6·2	5·8	10·6	8·5	0·2
1882	12·1	28·6	7·6	4·5	9·4	5·3	—
1883	4·7	16·6	13·8	2·6	4·6	19·0	—
1884	7·3	15·1	9·7	6·7	5·8	18·5	—
1885	3·4	14·1	7·1	4·7	11·0	14·9	—
1886	5·0	14·0	19·3	2·5	9·6	19·4	0·1
1887	12·9	23·9	18·9	1·5	10·5	16·5	0·2
1888	10·1	37·2	40·3	4·2	10·7	15·7	0·9
1889	11·2	37·2	40·2	8·9	11·2	14·2	—
1890	12·3	52·8	23·3	4·6	10·8	12·8	—
1891	5·0	18·7	9·4	6·6	5·7	12·3	0·4
1892	2·7	14·9	5·4	3·3	4·1	9·2	0·2
1893	1·7	13·1	5·4	2·6	2·5	6·7	0·2
1894	1·8	17·0	1·7	5·2	13·1	9·4	0·1
1895	3·6	26·0	4·1	14·9	10·4	18·7	—
1896	2·7	13·2	11·8	9·6	15·4	15·4	0·4
1897	8·1	16·7	4·9	10·8	27·2	10·7	—
1898	10·1	19·8	6·0	11·6	21·1	7·9	—
1899	8·6	12·1	5·9	21·3	21·7	7·0	1·5
1900	6·9	10·7	6·9	7·2	11·9	6·0	0·2
1901	5·8	14·1	6·7	9·2	4·6	9·1	0·1
1902	5·2	37·3	4·5	24·7	10·8	6·9	—
1903	2·1	17·3	11·3	42·4	6·6	3·0	0·2
1904	0·8	31·3	7·1	32·0	15·2	1·7	—
1905	3·0	43·9	13·2	29·9	35·6	3·3	—
1906	14·7	19·1	21·7	10·5	15·8	3·1	0·1
1907	7·0	42·7	30·2	9·5	23·4	3·3	0·2
1908	10·4	62·7	24·6	13·9	29·6	6·1	0·1
1909	13·6	68·4	38·6	18·7	25·4	10·5	0·4
1910	18·8	82·5	39·6	16·3	32·9	6·9	1·1
1911	14·5	73·5	38·5	9·4	24·7	8·4	0·1
1912	22·8	89·9	45·8	9·8	21·5	10·8	0·1
1913	18·9	116·9	36·2	8·1	17·4	18·8	1·2
1914	43·5	82·5	28·2	12·9	16·4	19·4	0·5

APPENDIX TABLE – (cont.)

	(II) By political status†		(III) By climate and ethnic group		
Year	Independent (8)	British Empire (9)	Regions of Rec. Set (10)	Tropics (11)	Other‡ (12)
1865	21·6	13·2	7·2	26·5	1·1
1866	17·0	8·1	7·7	12·8	0·2
1867	7·8	10·2	5·5	8·3	—
1868	16·9	12·2	6·6	10·8	—
1869	12·1	9·7	5·5	8·1	0·2
1870	33·9	9·9	12·1	12·5	1·5
1871	62·0	7·8	20·9	19·8	0·2
1872	84·4	7·3	36·1	22·7	0·1
1873	58·3	9·9	35·4	5·5	2·8
1874	53·2	20·9	40·9	8·5	—
1875	27·2	18·6	21·3	14·6	—
1876	12·0	18·4	2·0	5·7	0·3
1877	6·2	13·2	8·5	6·9	0·4
1878	13·6	17·6	18·0	6·6	1·0
1879	9·6	20·8	22·4	4·7	—
1880	22·6	18·7	32·7	6·1	0·3
1881	47·0	25·8	36·1	16·5	0·3
1882	44·7	21·8	39·6	15·0	0·9
1883	33·9	26·1	42·5	11·4	1·8
1884	27·6	35·2	47·6	8·0	—
1885	17·3	35·1	35·2	12·4	4·2
1886	32·1	34·8	43·8	20·4	0·6
1887	55·9	27·9	55·2	15·7	0·6
1888	75·9	42·0	79·8	27·9	1·3
1889	87·4	30·6	83·1	26·4	2·5
1890	85·7	28·6	86·4	15·3	2·2
1891	30·4	25·9	42·3	7·1	2·9
1892	19·7	19·0	29·4	6·7	1·1
1893	15·6	15·9	21·9	8·0	0·3
1894	20·1	27·7	28·1	15·9	2·7
1895	43·8	33·4	54·0	14·7	5·4
1896	38·0	29·9	42·3	17·5	6·1
1897	35·8	42·0	33·4	31·1	5·9
1898	44·2	31·8	38·2	21·0	2·3
1899	40·9	34·0	31·8	26·0	11·8
1900	20·3	25·7	24·7	16·0	2·0
1901	24·7	24·0	31·0	12·1	0·7
1902	45·9	42·1	64·4	15·1	3·5
1903	32·5	49·6	64·1	12·5	4·1
1904	43·9	43·9	58·4	18·8	9·9
1905	74·0	54·3	74·1	23·6	28·2
1906	57·2	25·2	35·1	23·8	11·6
1907	80·3	33·2	71·6	30·4	6·9
1908	77·5	68·4	89·0	42·8	5·2

APPENDIX TABLE – (cont.)

	(II) By political status†		(III) By climate and ethnic group		
Year	Independent (8)	British Empire (9)	Regions of Rec. Set (10)	Tropics (11)	Other ‡ (12)
1909	99·8	71·1	109·7	42·7	8·8
1910	105·3	81·3	106·7	68·7	3·0
1911	107·9	57·4	97·1	44·2	12·4
1912	123·5	66·3	125·6	39·0	9·2
1913	126·9	82·9	148·0	41·1	8·4
1914	103·7	90·9	129·2	29·0·	1·4

	(IV) By sector of issuer§			(V) By type of issuer		
Year	Social Overhead‖ (13)	Extractive¶ (14)	Mfg. (15)	Private (16)	Mixed** (17)	Gov't. (18)
1865	30·2	2·2	0·5	19·2	9·0	14·3
1866	15·4	1·1	0·1	10·5	5·1	9·8
1867	12·2	0·6	0·1	3·2	7·7	7·5
1868	26·3	0·9	0·1	4·5	13·5	11·2
1869	18·6	1·4	0·1	5·9	8·1	8·0
1870	29·9	5·6	—	14·7	6·5	23·5
1871	46·4	5·1	0·4	14·5	6·4	49·3
1872	66·2	7·0	1·1	41·4	4·5	47·9
1873	51·1	3·4	1·0	37·3	5·1	26·8
1874	65·0	3·8	0·7	28·7	7·8	38·0
1875	42·4	1·0	0·6	13·3	3·7	29·2
1876	27·1	0·6	0·3	9·2	0·8	20·6
1877	15·2	1·0	0·2	4·4	1·9	13·2
1878	22·7	0·8	0·6	9·8	2·3	19·6
1879	24·0	0·5	—	9·7	1·9	18·8
1880	33·9	4·6	0·2	26·3	2·0	13·4
1881	42·5	9·8	1·1	39·5	3·7	31·0
1882	45·5	4·4	1·7	35·5	13·0	19·0
1883	40·0	3·8	1·3	32·0	7·4	21·8
1884	41·6	6·3	0·7	23·9	9·2	29·8
1885	48·0	1·6	0·3	13·6	11·0	30·7
1886	59·4	6·1	0·6	19·5	12·8	37·5
1887	65·8	9·3	1·7	40·9	23·3	20·3
1888	89·8	8·9	2·7	48·5	17·1	53·5
1889	74·4	14·2	12·2	77·8	17·4	27·8
1890	70·2	8·4	18·2	86·6	9·1	20·8
1891	36·0	5·7	2·2	31·7	6·4	19·5
1892	28·7	4·2	2·9	20·7	3·5	15·6
1893	25·6	2·7	0·2	17·1	4·6	10·5
1894	35·2	5·3	0·9	19·1	6·1	23·1
1895	32·8	20·9	2·9	47·4	2·4	27·9

APPENDIX TABLE – *(cont.)*

| Year | (IV) By sector of issuer§ | | | (V) By type of issuer | | |
	Social Overhead‖ (13)	Extractive¶ (14)	Mfg. (15)	Private (16)	Mixed** (17)	Gov't. (18)
1896	31·2	23·9	1·6	41·0	8·7	18·8
1897	34·0	18·3	3·3	44·7	5·4	28·3
1898	43·7	15·4	5·7	45·3	5·4	25·9
1899	43·1	25·3	3·6	45·4	7·8	25·0
1900	31·9	9·9	1·2	29·3	4·0	16·2
1901	34·9	10·0	2·0	33·5	2·0	14·0
1902	68·1	13·7	2·1	62·0	3·8	23·4
1903	37·8	8·7	2·4	38·4	1·7	42·8
1904	55·5	8·5	1·6	46·0	3·7	38·3
1905	80·7	11·2	1·7	68·6	11·9	48·4
1906	43·7	14·1	2·9	54·7	5·5	24·7
1907	87·5	12.4	1·8	80·4	4·7	31·2
1908	122·4	9·1	4·6	76·1	13·7	57·6
1909	135·7	21·5	7·4	102·0	15·1	58·6
1910	121·5	51·8	4·7	136·6	13·4	48·0
1911	116·7	28·8	7·1	116·6	16·3	36·2
1912	130·4	24·2	21·1	152·4	5·9	42·4
1913	170·6	17·0	6·3	139·4	16·2	61·9
1914	176·4	9·5	5·7	90·6	17·1	95·5

* The classification by continent presents data on seven continents but excludes figures on multi-national transactions that could not be allocated to continents or countries.

† The classification by political status presents data for independent nations and the British Empire. It omits the statistics for foreign dependencies.

‡ Refers to non-tropical Asia.

§ The classification by sector of issuer includes those groupings which are directly relevant to problems of economic development. The following categories are excluded: finance and real estate, defence, and miscellaneous.

‖ Refers to the sum of transportation, public utilities, and other forms of public works.

¶ Refers to the sum of agriculture (including forestry) and mining.

** The 'mixed' category in the type of issuer classification is a heterogeneous group that includes issues by private enterprises that receive governmental assistance in the form of interest guarantees, etc.

investment. Of equal importance is the need to carry on external analysis by mobilizing related data on foreign trade, national income, public debts, security prices, and yields in order to test the validity of variants of both the classical and the income approach to the theory of international capital movements. In short, the agenda to continue the systematic exploration of the causes and effects of pre-1914 foreign investment including its relationship to economic development, more than a half century after the event, poses challenging possibilities.

ACKNOWLEDGEMENTS

The costs of machine time, programming, research assistance, and key punching were financed by grants from The Social Science Research Council and The Graduate School of Business Administration of New York University.

The use of the IBM-7094 computer and auxiliary equipment on a liberal basis was authorized by Professor Eugene Isaacson of The Institute of Mathematical Sciences of New York University. I am very grateful to him, to Henry Mullish for arranging and to Roger Beyar for completing the operations on the electronic computer.

I am especially obligated to Emanuel Mehr of the Geo-Physics Laboratory of New York University for revising and elaborating the original computer programme and testing and 'de-bugging' the new one.

My debt to Professor Leland H. Jenks for providing his files on pre-1914 new British foreign investment and affording many concrete suggestions on the technical problems of estimation is very great. His resources and insights transformed the character of this investigation.

Harvey H. Segal, my collaborator in the earlier phase of the project, has been a constant source of encouragement and advice. Valuable suggestions were made by David E. Novack, Laura Randall, Babette Solon, Irving Stone, and Brinley Thomas.

Professor Seymour Goodman of the Queens College Computer Center graciously authorized key-punching corrections, and the use of auxiliary equipment to prepare the data for final processing.

Lynn Alcosser prepared the charts. Research assistants, Leonard Mbogoa, Claire Pasternack, Martin Pollens, and Marvin Sporn performed a variety of laborious tasks. I owe a personal debt to Hyman Pasternack for his help in the final phase of this project.

2 Migration and International Investment

BRINLEY THOMAS

[This article was first published in B. Thomas (ed.) *The Economics of International Migration*, Macmillan, 1958.]

One of the interesting questions raised by the period ending in the 1920s is the nature of the mechanism by which the economies of the leading countries reacted on one another. The subject has recently attracted a good deal of attention, but much work remains to be done before a satisfactory account can be given. We shall begin by examining the part played by movements of population and capital in the growth of the international economy up to 1913. Was there an automatic mechanism guaranteeing relative stability as long as migration continued? What are the main contrasts between the trends since 1945 and those of the nineteenth century? Is the rupture of the old relationship between international investment and international migration a cause of instability?

1 The Pattern before 1913

1 MIGRATION AND THE FLOW OF CAPITAL. There were two well-marked phases in the evolution of British foreign lending up to 1913. In the first phase, ending in the sixties, there was a good deal of lending to governments; about three-fifths of the £785 million of British investments abroad in 1870 were in government bonds, and much of that money had gone into military rather than economic enterprises. Another feature of the earlier part of the century was the great outburst of direct investment on the continent of Europe by British entrepreneurs, for whom it was a matter of pride as well as profit to

be able to export the industrial revolution. This activity entailed the temporary emigration from the United Kingdom of technicians and other labour required to build the new capital equipment.[1]

In the second phase British loanable funds went for the most

TABLE I *Peaks and Troughs in British Foreign Lending and European Oversea Emigration, 1860–1913*

United Kingdom net income available for foreign investment*		European emigration to overseas countries†	
Trough year	Peak year	Trough year	Peak year
1862		1861	
	1872		1872
1877		1877	
	1890		1891
1898		1898	
	1908		1907

Sources: * A. H. Imlah, 'The Balance of Payments and the Export of Capital of the United Kingdom, 1816–1913', *Economic History Review*, Second Series, vol. v, no. 2, 1952, pp. 234–9. † G. Sundbärg's figures in *Emigrationsutredningen*, Bilaga iv, *Utvandringsstatistik*, Stockholm, 1910, pp. 102–3.

part into the purchase of securities in the underpopulated lands overseas. A clear and significant pattern may be seen in the population and capital flows of the period 1860–1913; each of the three upsurges in immigration from Europe – 1863–72, 1879–91, and 1898–1901 – was accompanied by a boom in British capital exports. That international migration synchronized almost exactly with international investment is evident from Table I.

In 1913 aggregate British foreign investment amounted to

[1] The most famous of these capital exporters was Thomas Brassey. 'He financed more than one banking house as a means to secure emergency credit. Eighty thousand men were at one time in his employ. English schools, priests, chapels, and physicians followed their migration from one contract to the next. To keep such an organization employed agents and partners roved the commercialized world seeking opportunities and concessions. At one time Brassey had railways and docks under construction in five continents. Every country in Europe possesses a specimen of this craft with the possible exception of Greece, Albania and Finland. In his thirty-five years of business life he was engaged upon one hundred and seventy different contracts, involving nearly eight thousand miles of railway.' – L. H. Jenks *The Migration of British Capital to 1875.* Cape, 1938, pp. 136–7.

£3763 million distributed geographically as follows: 47 per cent in the British Empire, 20 per cent in the United States, 20 per cent in Latin America, and only 6 per cent in Europe. The destinations of the 24 million European emigrants in the years 1891–1914 were roughly as follows: 54 per cent to the United States, 25 per cent to Latin America, and 17 per cent to the British Empire. This simple picture of labour and capital flowing from a crowded continent to the underdeveloped sector of the world becomes more complicated when we examine the process closely.

2 MIGRATION AND INVERSE INVESTMENT CYCLES. From the 1840s to the eve of the First World War the long swings in the economic development of the United Kingdom and the United States were inverse to one another; and this coincided with a one-way traffic of capital and labour across the Atlantic. Some of the relevant data are summarized in Table II for the period 1869–1913. We are fortunate that for these years we have for both countries fairly reliable statistics of the national income and capital formation. The long swings (with a span of about eighteen to twenty years) in home investment in the United Kingdom and the United States show an inverse relation.

The alternating phases suggest an intercontinental rivalry for resources. A wave of investment in construction did not take place on both sides of the Atlantic at the same time; the lender gave way to the borrower and later the borrower did likewise for the lender. For Great Britain the process undoubtedly entailed relative long-run stability in the level of production, since the home construction and export sectors offset each other. This was not true of the United States, for there the magnitudes of the two sectors were different; in the period 1869–1913 merchandise imports averaged about 30 per cent of the net national product in Great Britain and only 6 per cent in the United States. Over the long period the world's leading creditor kept putting its money back into circulation – through vigorous foreign lending in one phase and a considerable expansion in its imports of primary produce in the next phase.

The absence of a chronic sterling shortage was due, not to any superior wisdom on the part of the British, but to the inner compulsions of the British economy and the relation between its growth and that of the then underdeveloped countries. Intercontinental mobility of population and capital was indispensable to the economic development of the new lands; and the rhythmic movement of these flows was a necessary

TABLE 11 *The United States and the United Kingdom: Rates of Change in Migration, Investment, and Real Income* per capita *from Decade to Overlapping Decade, 1869–1913*

United States

Decade (Yearly average)	Total immigration	Net immigration from U.K.	Net Producer durables	Net construction	Real income per capita
	%	%	%	%	%
1869–78	—	—	—	—	—
1874–83	+26·4	+104·0	+73·5	+39·0	+29·3
1879–88	+35·1	+ 74·4	+27·7	+53·6	+17·3
1884–93	− 4·4	− 18·7	− 4·2	+56·3	+ 5·5
1889–98	−19·7	− 37·9	− 7·7	+19·7	+ 3·8
1894–1903	+ 7·2	− 29·8	+49·2	− 3·1	+42·3
1899–1908	+89·3	+ 41·4	+75·3	+15·8	+14·2
1904–13	+25·2	+ 4·7	+ 9·4	+14·6	+ 9·6

United Kingdom

Decade (Yearly average)	Volume of home investment	Volume of building	Balance of Payments on Income Account	Unemployment	Real income per capita
	%	%	%	%	%
1869–78	—	—	—	—	—
1874–83	+12·8	+12·8	− 50·4	+50·0	+ 5·3
1879–88	− 4·8	−13·5	+102·1	+44·4	+ 8·6
1884–93	+ 6·2	− 2·1	+ 46·6	− 4·6	+14·2
1889–98	+24·3	+23·7	− 25·4	−29·0	+11·6
1894–1903	+26·3	+30·3	− 37·6	−11·4	+ 7·0
1899–1908	+10·1	+ 5·2	+120·3	+10·3	+ 2·9
1904–13	− 5·5	−22·1	+132·4	+ 9·3	+ 2·8

Source: Brinley Thomas, *Migration and Economic Growth*, National Institute of Economic and Social Research Study, Cambridge University Press, 1954, pp. 111–13 and references cited there.

condition of the relative long-run stability in British industrial production.

The analysis suggests that, where a highly industrialized creditor country is a heavy importer of food and raw materials from an under-populated debtor country to which it exports labour and capital goods, there is a presumption that the growth of the two economies will involve inverse fluctuations in home investment and consequent disharmonious rates of economic growth.

3 THE WORKING OF THE INTERNATIONAL MECHANISM. The inverse relation between construction cycles was true not only of Great Britain and the United States but also of Great Britain and other debtor countries – Australia, Canada, and Argentina. For example, statistics of railway building and brick production in Australia reveal a prominent boom in the eighties when immigration and capital imports from Britain were heavy, a downswing in the nineties corresponding to a boom in capital formation in Britain, and another upsurge in activity in the early years of this century when British Funds and emigrants were again pouring in.

Any attempt to throw light on this interaction must start from the hypothesis that, to quote Professor Viner, '. . . major long-term capital movements have . . . mainly been "disturbing" rather than "equilibrating" in character'.[1] It does not go to the root of the matter to say, as Professor Cairncross does, that '. . . it was upon the terms of trade that the distribution of investment between home and foreign, as well as the course of real wages, ultimately depended'.[2] Space does not allow a discussion of this question here. Cairncross has to go out of his way to find reasons why heavy British capital exports in the eighties should have coincided with a *deterioration* in the terms of trade of the borrowing countries, for the link seemed to work so well in the nineties and the 1900s. Before we can reach a firm conclusion there is need for much more detailed

[1] J. Viner, *Studies in the Theory of International Trade*, Allen & Unwin, p. 365.
[2] A. K. Cairncross, *Home and Foreign Investment, 1870–1913*, Cambridge University Press, 1953, p. 208.

analysis of the time series. The background of what follows, however, is that movements in the terms of trade are to be looked upon more as consequences than as causal forces.

A broad picture of the process can be given in the following terms. Let us envisage a simple international economy consisting of a creditor and debtor country similar to the United Kingdom and the United States in the middle of the last century. In each there is a home construction and an export sector. Over the long period the sectors within each country compete for resources, and the two countries compete for the resources of the economy which they comprise. Let C be the highly industrialized creditor country and D the under-populated debtor country rich in natural resources.

Let us suppose that in Period 1 a large outflow of population takes place from C to D. This immigration brings about in D an induced wave of fixed capital formation (e.g. railways and housing) financed initially by an extension of credit; this in turn induces an inflow of loanable funds from C. D has a strong propensity to spend its borrowings on C's capital goods, so the export sector in C (which we assume to be fairly large in relation to national income) gets a boom which is at the expense of home construction. The departure of migrants has reduced the demand for housing and other fixed capital in C, and loanable funds flow out to take advantage of the marginal efficiency of fixed investment in D.

Thus in Period 1 there is a construction boom in D and an export boom in C induced by the flow of population and capital. What happens to the price structures? Inflationary expansion (accompanied by speculation) in D sucks labour and resources into construction at the expense of D's export sector; the full effect of this is reflected in the domestic price level. The prices of domestic goods rise most; next to them come export prices; the prices of imports rise least.[1] An important determinant of the latter is the fact that C can draw factors easily into its export sector from the depressed construction sector, and so its expansion can proceed for some

---

[1] Cf. the experience of Canada, 1910–13. See Cairncross, *Home and Foreign Investment, 1870–1913*, ch. 3.

time without any rise in costs. Booming exports accompanied by depressed constructional activity yield a more moderate expansion than booming constructional activity accompanied by depressed exports. Thus the net barter terms of trade, i.e. the ratio of export prices to import prices, move against C and in favour of D.

The crucial question is: what brings Period 1 to an end? This raises all the complexities of the theory of cyclical downturn. All we need to do here is to suggest that, if investment is a function of the relation of output to capacity, the boom in D, being of a more inflationary character, will be the first to reach its ceiling. C investors, influenced by the narrowing margin between the profitability of foreign and home investment (and the increasing risk attached to the former), switch loanable funds into home construction. The flow of emigrants reacts in sympathy.

In Period 2 we have the reverse process – an expansion in home construction in C and in exports in D, and a recession in capital and labour migration. The productive capacity of D's export sector in Period 2 is directly related to the expansion that took place in its capital equipment in Period 1; a substantial supply of primary produce is exported at falling or only slowly rising prices. Meanwhile C gets a vigorous construction boom, with a rapid increase in the volume of imports; the net barter terms of trade are now in favour of C and against D. The mechanism here is that the output capacity of primary produce in D is much increased as a consequence of the investment in fixed capital there in Period 1; whereas in C in Period 2 there is a shift away from its export sector to home construction and this tends to make its export goods relatively dearer. If farmers in the debtor country are hit by the adverse terms of trade in Period 2, that is part of the price they have to pay for having railways and houses built at a rapid rate in the previous period with the aid of men and money from abroad. One cannot expect to gain on the swings *and* the roundabouts![1] Each

---

[1] Contrast the view of P. J. O'Leary and W. Arthur Lewis: 'Whatever may have been the cause of the secular fluctuation in the export of capital, its effect on the dependent overseas economies was deplorable from their point of view,

country, creditor as well as debtor, in its home construction boom period lays the foundations for the performance of its export sector in the following period. Moreover, during export booms there is a shift away from construction investment to investment in producers' goods, the demand for which is sensitive to the level of activity in the export sector. There is, thus, an alternation of minor secular booms in fixed capital investment in the lending and borrowing countries; and it is during these booms that each country experiences its most rapid rate of growth of real income per head.

The above sketch is merely an outline of a possible interpretation of the role of capital and labour flows in the nineteenth century. It is very difficult to obtain a statistical measure of the sequence of events at the turning-points of the minor secular swings. A very rough attempt made on British data in the period 1860–1910 suggested that upturns in home construction preceded downturns in the export sector, whereas upturns in the export sector (American railway investment and/or emigration) preceded downturns in home construction.[1]

Statistical analysis of lags suggests that up to the sixties the pace of activity in the United States was conditioned by the inflow of migrants and capital from Europe, but that in the subsequent period the immigration waves were determined by the course of American investment in producer durables, while building activity continued to lag after immigration. There is ample evidence that fluctuations in the net migration balance were an important variable in the long swings in the growth of the American economy; they exercised a strong influence on changes in the rate of growth of the American population.

Some writers throw doubt on the whole idea of an interplay

---

since it transmitted to them a secular fluctuation in investment and output which was not necessarily even related to demand: on the contrary, their capacity to produce built up most during the prolonged slump in prices from 1883 to 1896. . . . If there was an automatic mechanism for stabilising the U.K. economy, by its very nature this was a mechanism for destabilising the rest of the world.' – 'Secular Swings in Production and Trade', *The Manchester School*, May 1955, p. 146.

[1] See Brinley Thomas, op. cit., p. 186.

between the economies of Great Britain and the United States. Mr O'Leary and Professor Arthur Lewis, intrigued by the inverse relation and sceptical of the influence of migration and capital flows, confess that they '. . . cannot even rule out the possibility that the alternation of the U.S. and U.K. building cycles was a sheer accident, springing perhaps from the different effects which the Napoleonic Wars may have had upon the progress of residential building in the two countries'.[1] This is surely to throw up the sponge too soon. The arguments with which these authors dismiss the role of migration and investment fail to carry conviction. They contend that British lending could have had little effect on capital formation in America, because the latter's capital imports were insignificant in relation to its own savings – 'averaging between 1874 and 1895 less than a half of one per cent of gross national product'.[2] The same kind of argument is used against migration as a possible link between the economies of the United Kingdom and the United States: '. . . differences in emigration rates made less than a quarter of one per cent difference to the annual rate of growth of population, so one treats this explanation with suspicion'.[3] Obviously if you express migration and capital flows as a proportion of population growth and gross national product respectively, you will nearly always get ridiculously small percentages; but these percentages are irrelevant. It is surely the margin that counts. What we have to look at is the key industry or sector which sets the pace in each phase of rapid growth, and consider the relative significance of capital inflow to that sector. In the upswing of 1866–73 the railway mileage of the United States was doubled; this was entirely financed (directly or indirectly) through the import of 2 billion dollars of foreign funds. As L. H. Jenks pointed out: 'British, Dutch and German investors were then buying nearly half of the Civil War debt . . . to the amount of more than a billion dollars par. The railroads obtained directly only about half a billion. The purchase of government bonds by foreigners,

---

[1] P. J. O'Leary and W. Arthur Lewis, loc. cit., p. 127.
[2] Loc. cit., p. 125.
[3] Loc. cit., p. 126.

however, released savings and bank resources for railway, industrial, and commercial promotion in the United States.'[1]

Furthermore, the impact of capital inflow must not be taken in isolation: those big inflows were always accompanied by immigration. Throughout the period 1840–1924 building activity in the United States consistently lagged a year or two behind immigration (there was only one exception – in the seventies).[2] The two together, railway construction and residential building, highly sensitive to change in the rate of growth of population, made up a large portion of current capital formation. And then, of course, there was the multiplier.[3] Mr O'Leary and Professor Lewis have hardly justified their conclusion that '. . . the U.S. governed its own fortunes in the nineteenth century and if any adjustment had to be made it was made on the other side of the Atlantic'.[4] Their scepticism about the effect of emigration on the building cycle in Great Britain seems at first sight a little more plausible; but here again the simple percentage is not a very reliable guide. A slump in emigration meant (*a*) an increase in population concentrated in the house-seeking age group, and (*b*) a substantial increase in internal migration to the industrial areas stimulated by the rise in home investment; both these factors had a direct bearing on the demand for housing. Moreover, a decline in emigration was accompanied by a rise in the volume of loanable funds available at home.

[1] L. H. Jenks, 'Railroads as an Economic Force in American Development', *Enterprise and Social Change*, ed. F. C. Lane and J. C. Riemersma, Allen & Unwin, 1953, p. 169.

[2] See Brinley Thomas, op. cit., ch. 10.

[3] 'The construction moment of railway history brought an initial demand for . . . durable goods. Hence there was a chance for the innovator in the lumbering industry, in quarries, in iron mills and carriage works. Indeed these industries were hard put to keep pace with railway construction. Until the later eighties, every boom period found American factories unable to meet the demand for rails, and there were heavy importations from England and Wales. As late as the nineties, over one-fifth of the total output of pig iron in the United States was being rolled into railroad bars. Much of this demand for durable goods turned eventually into a demand for labor in mine and quarry and mill, into wage payment of labor. . . . Thus the initial impetus of investment in railway construction led in widening arcs to increments of economic activity over the entire American domain, far exceeding in their total volume the original inputs of investment capital.' – Jenks, loc. cit., pp. 166–7.   [4] Loc. cit.

3 The Long Swing: Comparisons and Interactions Between British and American Balance of Payments, 1820–1913[1]

JEFFREY G. WILLIAMSON

[This article was first published in *The Journal of Economic History*, Vol. XXII, No. 1. (1962).]

In the past decade there has been an extremely active interest in the evidence and importance of the twenty-year building cycle, or Kuznets cycle as Lewis suggests we call it, in both American nineteenth-century development and British development after 1870.[2] The evidence of building cycles in the United States is perhaps more extensive and seems clearly, in the research accumulated by Kuznets, Burns, and Abramovitz, to indicate a long swing in the general process of growth, not just long swings isolated to the building trades.[3] Whereas American long

[1] Estimates and calculations not documented are from my unpublished research into the effects of the long swing upon the United States balance of payments. I wish to express my thanks to Moses Abramovitz for inestimable advice.

[2] See for instance: R. C. O. Matthews, *The Business Cycle* (Chicago: The University of Chicago Press, 1959), especially Chapter 12; Moses Abramovitz, 'Resource and Output Trends in the United States since 1870', *American Economic Review*, XLVI, No. 2 (May 1956), 5–24; Brinley Thomas, *Migration and Economic Growth* (Cambridge: The University Press, 1954); and most recently, E. W. Cooney, 'Long Waves in Building in the British Economy of the Nineteenth Century', *The Economic Histor Review*, Second Series, XIII (December 1960), 257–69.

[3] Simon Kuznets, *Long Term Changes in National Income of the United States since 1869*, Income and Wealth. Series II, published for the International Association for Research in Income and Wealth (Cambridge: Bowes and Bowes, 1952); Moses Abramovitz' work is most recently summarized in *The Nature and Significance of Kuznets Cycles*, mimeographed for the Stanford Research Center in Economic Growth (December 1960), and which appeared in *Economic Development and Cultural Change*, IX, No. 3 (April 1961), 225–48; Arthur Burns, *Production Trends in the United States Since 1870* (New York: National Bureau of Economic Research, 1934).

C

swings pervade all domestic series of output, income, and investment, British experience seems somewhat different. After 1870 long swings in British capital exports alternated with long swings in domestic investment in a fashion which eliminated excess fluctuations in income and output, which would have been due mainly to fluctuations in aggregate demand.[1]

Most of these investigations into long swings in the process of development concern domestic movements; their evidence in American development extends back into the nineteenth century at least as far as the 1820s, while significant evidence of these swings in British history seems to be available only after 1870. Apart from one recent exception,[2] no important attempts have been made to extend the Kuznets cycle analysis to encompass the international flow of goods, capital, and specie, although there has been an investigation of swings in labour migration, most notably by Thomas. Surely one important reason for the lack of attention to this aspect of the long swing has been due to the unavailability of net capital flow estimates. This statistical gap has been filled quite recently with research done by Douglass C. North, Matthew Simon, and Albert H. Imlah.[3]

The purpose of this paper is not primarily to examine long

[1] This relationship has perhaps been most energetically pursued by A. K. Cairncross, *Home and Foreign Investment, 1870–1913* (Cambridge: The University Press, 1953); Thomas, *Migration and Economic Growth;* and W. A. Lewis and P. J. O'Leary, 'Secular Swings in Production and Trade, 1870–1913', *The Manchester School of Economic and Social Studies*, XIII (May 1955), 113–52.

[2] Douglass C. North, *The Economic Growth of the United States, 1790–1860* (Englewood Cliffs, N.J.: Prentice-Hall, Inc., 1961). This excellent little book appeared after this manuscript was completed.

[3] Douglass C. North, 'The United States Balance of Payments, 1790–1860', *Trends in the American Economy in the Nineteenth Century*. Studies in Income and Wealth, Vol. 24, pf the National Bureau of Economic Research (Princeton: Princeton University Press, 1960), pp. 573–627; Matthew Simon, 'The United States Balance of Payments, 1861–1900', *Trends*, pp. 629–715; Albert H. Imlah, *Economic Elements in the Pax Britannica* (Cambridge, Mass.: Harvard University Press, 1958).

In the research contained in this paper I have used North's and Simon's estimates to cover nineteenth-century United States and Imlah's estimates for British balance of payments 1820–1913. The estimates for net capital movements over United States borders from 1901–13 are taken from Raymond W. Goldsmith, *A Study of Saving in the United States* (3 vols; Princeton: Princeton University Press, 1955), I, 1078–93, Tables K-1 through K-7.

swings in the United States balance of payments. Although I will review the evidence of long swings in the flow of international capital, goods, and specie in American nineteenth-century history, my major goal here will be an examination of two aspects of their evidence in British balance of payments. First, did the domestic long-swing mechanism produce similar movements in British capital exports, merchandise imports, and merchandise exports with the same violence that was exhibited in American movements? The first purpose of this paper, then, is a comparison of the effects of a domestic long swing upon the international transactions of a relatively developed, high-income, chronic capital exporter with the balance of payments movements of a relatively under-developed, capital-scarce, net capital importer undergoing these same internal swings in the process of growth. Very little research has been devoted to British experience with long swings in the balance of payments prior to 1870, and the analysis of the nineteenth century in the literature as a whole has not been very systematic. Second, and perhaps even more interesting, what is the mechanism of interaction between these two members of the nineteenth-century Atlantic economy? Is there a *systematic* relationship between British and American development in the nature of an inverse Kuznets cycle, and is it possible that this interrelated mechanism had its source in one of the two countries? And finally, if a *systematic* inverse relation between the rate of domestic growth of Great Britain and America did indeed exist, did it arise predominantly from independent internal conditions or by the direct effects of fluctuating international demands for, and supplies of, goods, securities and specie or by the indirect effects of labour migration? These are some of the major questions towards which this paper will be directed.

American demands for goods from, and in part supplies of goods to, the international market do indeed reveal long swings as early as 1820, and are clearly evident without the sometimes questionable methods of moving averages, trend removal, and calculated rates of change. The movements are easily identifiable in the unadulterated annual estimates. Over the nineteenth century as a whole imports of goods into the United States are positively related to composite dating of Kuznets cycles in domestic activity, and after 1860 deflated imports reveal an extremely high positive correlation with income, output, and investment series; that is, from 1830–70, deflated imports are positively related to the Riggleman building index with $r = 0.95$; from 1860–1900, deflated imports are positively related to the Fickey index of manufacturing production and railroad mileage added where $r = 0.822$ and $r = 0.938$ respectively; and from 1890–1914, deflated imports are positively related to the Riggleman building index, $r = 0.871$, and railroad mileage added, $r = 0.903$.[1] Without exception the fluctuations in American imports over the Kuznets cycle in domestic growth had more violent amplitude than export movements. Imports dominated the trade balance from 1820–1913, with exports only randomly affecting the timing and amplitude of the trade balance. During periods of extremely rapid growth, on the upswing of a Kuznets cycle, the trade balance became progressively worse, reflecting increasing excess demands for goods in the domestic system. These periods of worsening in the trade balance alternated with periods of improvement, when domestic growth was sluggish or more seriously involved with protracted periods of deficiencies in aggregate demand.

This description of a Kuznets cycle in merchandise imports, which also reflects itself in the balance of trade, slights the importance of the export market in *conditioning* the pace of American development prior to the Civil War. Although they were less severe in amplitude, before 1860 exports also exhibited long secular swings positively related to the pace of domestic growth. Indeed, in its undeveloped state our development was very much a function of conditions in the export market: a market dominated by cotton and, to a lesser extent, grain. Some have supported the view that the long swing in

[1] In these tests, both series were smoothed by a five-year moving average after their trends has been removed by

$$\log y = \alpha_0 - \alpha_1 t - \alpha_2 t^2.$$

American development (during a period of export monopoly) was *initiated* by a persistent and endogenous lag of raw material and foodstuff production behind supply price.[1] In other research which is not reviewed here, I found no evidence which would throw doubt on this thesis. On the contrary, any new evidence which I compiled strongly supports the view that long swings in the American economy prior to the 1850s could be explained by fluctuations in export supply as described above.[2] Nevertheless, at the end of the American Civil War, after a period of secular transition, export movements no longer displayed similar long swings, and over the nineteenth century as a whole they did not interfere with the singular importance of imports in dictàting the state of the trade balance.

Concomitant with alternation in the pace of real growth over the long swing and alternating excess demands for goods reflected in the trade balance, there must have been variations in (ex-ante) excess demands for money as well. During periods of rapid growth in income and output, tendencies towards heavy excess demands for increments in real money balances are the rule, while during periods of sluggish growth and prolonged depressions the tendency may be even towards an excess supply. Under a nineteenth-century gold standard system, how was it possible to eliminate price deflation and/or serious deficiencies in aggregate demand which could have interfered with maximum growth performance over the long swing? In the face of an increasingly unfavourable trade balance during periods of rapid growth and concomitant import demand, how was it possible to eliminate gold outflow

---

[1] Douglass C. North has presented this argument most cogently, an argument to which I also subscribe, in 'Location Theory and Regional Economic Growth', *Journal of Political Economy*, LXIII, No. 3 (June 1955), 243–58; 'Agriculture and Regional Economic Growth', American Farm Economic Association *Proceedings*, XLI, No. 5 (Dec. 1959), 943–51; 'International Capital Flows and the Development of the American West,' *The Journal of Economic History*, XVI, No. 4 (December 1956), 493–505; *The Economic Growth of the United States, 1790–1860*.

[2] See also my note in a recent issue of this *Journal*, 'International Trade and United States Economic Development: 1827–1843', *The Journal of Economic History*, XXI, No. 3 (September 1961), 372–83.

and cause an inflow of specie as well, when under 'normal' conditions an internal supply of gold was insufficient to satisfy excess demands for money? There is evidence that prior to the western gold discoveries, 1820–50, and after the Resumption, 1879–1914, there was a long swing in the rate of inflow of gold positively related to income growth and postulated excess demands for real money balances; there is also evidence that during the period 1879–1904, at least, the external flow of gold was primary in determining the rate of growth of the money supply.

Extensive periods of rapid development were accompanied by rising net capital imports during upswings in Kuznets cycles – so much so that fluctuations in the trade balance were overshadowed by this flow of American securities abroad. Long swings in the rate of net capital import are perhaps the most obvious evidence of long swings in balance of payments. The kinds of securities which foreigners, mainly British, were induced to purchase when every acceleration in the pace of development created an increasingly unfavourable trade balance were particularly of one type. From 1820–1913, about three fifths to four fifths of all American securities accepted abroad were either state and municipal bonds (used to finance a developing transportation network) or railroad stocks and bonds. Trade deficits generated during periods of rapid growth were financed, then, by systematic recurrences in transportation development positively related to (causing?) rates of income and output growth.

We have in American experience Kuznets cycles in our balance of payments. The flow of goods, capital, and specie (and, of course, labour migration) exhibit definite long swings over the course of American development. Their dating in terms of peaks and troughs is given in Table I, and the movements in net capital imports can be seen in Chart 5.

There are two excellent justifications for a simultaneous examination of British balance of payments with an investigation of domestic long swings and their effects upon American trade. First, since there is preliminary evidence of a long swing in many British domestic series *after* 1870, and especially in home investment,[1] it seemed fruitful to study British experience to throw further light upon the question of Kuznets cycles and their effect upon the international flow of goods, capital, and specie.

Realistically, we should be prepared for different secular movements in the balance of payments of an important capital

TABLE 1 *U.S. Balance of Payments Dating for Long Swings: 1817–1917 (Smoothed Data)**

	Imports (current value)	Imports (deflated)	Net Capital Inflow (current value)		Trade Balance (current value)		Exports (current value)	Exports (deflated)
Peak	1817	—	1817	Trough	1817	Peak	1818	1832
Trough	1822	1822	1825	Peak	1825	Trough	1822	1835
Peak	1837	1837	1837	Trough	1837	Peak	1838	1847
Trough	1842	1842	1842	Peak	1842	Trough	1844	1848
Peak	1858	1859	1852	Trough	1855	Peak	1858	1860
Trough	1863	1863	1858	Peak	1860	Trough	1863	1863
Peak	1873	1874	1871	Trough	1871	Peak		
Trough	1877	1877	1879	Peak	1879	Trough		
Peak	1891	1895	1888	Trough	1888	Peak		
Trough	1896	1896	1900	Peak	1900	Trough		
Peak	1915	1915	1911	Trough	1908	Peak		

* Although these dates are for the series after smoothing by a five-year moving average, there is no significant difference between those and the dates for peak and trough derived from the annual data.

exporter compared with those of a chronic capital importer, even when faced with the evidence of internal long swings in both the lending and receiving nations. But as in the relation between American internal development and her capital imports, British capital exports should exhibit an inverse relation with the pace of internal development or with domestic outlets for domestic savings; that is, when the pace of British internal development was low, English investors should have shifted increasingly to more lucrative investments abroad, just as when American business slowed there was a net reduction in capital imports or even a serious net export of capital. So much for similarities. Dissimilarities may arise for at least two major reasons. First, because of its resource endowment and small size, foreign trade played and does play a much greater

[1] As indicated earlier in this paper, Cairncross, Matthews, Lewis and O'Leary, and Thomas have shown the most interest in the evidence of long swings or Kuznets cycles in British home investment, as well as the apparent inversion between British home and foreign investment.

role in the British system than in the American. Thus, although British and American experience may *both* reflect an inverse relation between domestic and foreign investment over the Kuznets cycle, net foreign investment assumed a much more important role as a determinant in British than in American aggregate demand. Cairncross estimated that between 1875 and 1914 a little more than 40 per cent of British capital investment was in net capital exports, while in 1913, the share was as large as 50 per cent.[1] This averages about *three or four times* the American estimates; in the post-1860 period, the highest share of net capital imports in total capital accumulation was 27 per cent, while the average share from 1870–1900, *during periods of positive inflow alone*, lies between only 10–15 per cent.[2]

For these very reasons, and apart from relative internal conditions, we would anticipate much less violent fluctuations in aggregate output over the long swing in home investment, due to the offsetting effects of net capital exports on aggregate demand. British import demand should, therefore, reveal mild fluctuations since imports are generally written as some function of national output. In this respect, however, Cairncross, Lewis and O'Leary, and Matthews put the argument in much stronger terms than either Thomas or I would. Those authors imply that evidence of a long swing in British national output, and in all expenditures related to it, would be lacking. It seems more cautious, but more nearly correct, to suggest that a dampening of the domestic long swing likely occurred,

[1] Cairncross, *Home and Foreign Investment*, pp. 2, 4.

[2] Of course changes in net foreign investment would be more pertinent than absolute levels in determining the relative importance of capital movements as a stabilizing component of aggregate demand. However, American fluctuations in the import of capital were not so very much more violent than British variations in the export of capital. For that matter, it is also true that net capital flows are not precisely measures of net foreign investment.

Cairncross' estimates are consistent with some recent estimates of the importance of external trade (exports plus imports of goods) as a share in total income. Deutsch and Eckstein estimate that from 1860–1920 British external trade was from 50–60 per cent of national income. The same share in the United States was 15–20 per cent from 1819–1839 and 10–15 per cent from 1859–1909. K. W. Deutsch and A. Eckstein, 'National Industrialization and the Declining Share of the International Economic Sector, 1890–1959', *World Politics*, XIII (January 1961), 267–99.

and that severe depressions and excessive booms in aggregate demand at the troughs and peaks of long swings in the rate of development were more likely to be avoided. Although severe fluctuations in aggregate demand may have been cushioned over the long swing, this does not imply a constant growth path of capacity output, or that fluctuations in domestic investment were completely offset.

A second suspected difference between British and American balance of payments movements over the Kuznets cycle would lie in export movements. As a capital exporter, and especially under the assumption of mild import fluctuations, the rate of expansion of the export industry ought to be very closely related to the outflow of foreign capital – the real transfer should be facilitated mainly by export increments. Whereas American experience revealed import movements dominating the trade balance to facilitate the real transfer, we should expect that British trade-balance fluctuations were dominated by exports. And finally, since export movements should be inversely related to long swings in British home investment, the trade balance should have reached peak deficits at high levels of British home investment and at low levels of net capital exports – movements, though caused in a different manner, precisely like those found in United States experience.

Besides using this excursion into British balance of payments movements in a comparative manner, there is also a second and perhaps more pertinent justification for the research. I have attempted with some success to include conditions in Great Britain as an explanatory factor for American net capital imports,[1] but did American Kuznets cycles also have *direct* effects upon British economic conditions via movements in the balance of payments?[2] That is, did fluctuations in United States import demand have profound, and direct, effects upon total British exports, or was the American market too small, or did other developing nations take up the slack, or both? The problem can be re-worded more elegantly to ask whether or

[1] See footnote 2, p. 64.
[2] By *indirect*, I have in mind the effects of the migration of labour upon income and prices in both nations.

not the United States simultaneously created its own increasing supply of foreign capital on the upswing of a Kuznets cycle by dominating fluctuations in the rate of expansion of British export markets, and thereby creating a concomitant trade balance surplus in Great Britain; if not, then the interrelationship becomes much more subtle.

The second possible direct influence is via prices of traded goods. We may find that any evidence of a mild long swing in British import demands is eliminated by raw material and foodstuff price movements. If grain and cotton prices dominated British import price movements, American export prices in cotton and, to a lesser extent, grain may have had a profound influence upon British imports *in current prices* at least prior to 1860/1870. Prior to the 1860s, American export prices were positively related to domestic activity, while over the nineteenth century as a whole British and American internal development moved inversely. It is likely that British import demand moved inversely with American export prices, and thus it seems reasonable to expect that American export prices had a smoothing influence on British imports in current prices.[1]

Earlier research has made it clear that supply conditions of investment funds in Great Britain played an important role in determining the amplitude of American net capital imports.[2]

---

[1] United States imports and import prices exhibit a reasonably significant positive correlation over the long swing. This *may* be explained in the same manner since in this case American import demand and British export prices move in sympathy. Given our assumptions above, it is more likely that British imports and import prices move inversely.

[2] Although not in its timing, the amplitude of long swings in American net capital imports is in part explained by inverse conditions in Great Britain ('push'). In regression analysis to test the explanatory power of British and American stock prices in explaining United States net capital imports, when we include only American ('pull') conditions $R^2 = 0.624$ (1873–1914), but when we include conditions in both countries,

$$K^t = 112.42 + 420.71 \ P^{t-3} - 552.39 \ P^{t-2}, \ \overline{R}^2 = 0.83.$$
$$(64.41) \ US \quad (72.52) \ GB$$

The same results occur in the period 1844–1860; if we use only American stock prices, $\overline{R}^2 = 0.769$; if we include conditions in both countries, $\overline{R}^2 = 0.910$. These tests were done where K, net capital movements, and both P's, general stock prices in Great Britain and railroad stock prices in American, are trendless and smoothed.

The final direct effect of United States balance of payments upon British balance of payments might include the importance of American security markets in influencing British capital exports. It was not necessary that America's share of British capital export be large, only that its fluctuations in demand for British capital were excessive enough to dictate long swings in British capital exports.

It should be frankly admitted at the outset that this paper actually raises more questions than it answers, especially with regard to the framework of the Atlantic economy envisioned by Thomas or the broader interactions in nineteenth-century development of capital-scarce, agricultural, raw material-producing nations and capital-rich, manufactures-producing nations. The major question of the evidence of long swings in Australian, Argentine, Canadian, etc., development and international interactions over the course of nineteenth-century expansion must be deferred until a later time.

Our expectations concerning import movements are supported by the data.[1] Even after removing the trend, British imports in current prices reveal no evidence whatever of long swings. What trend removal *does* exhibit are longer movements associated with 'Kondratieff' swings in import prices. In the trendless series, British imports in current prices fall steadily for about twenty years from the mid-twenties to the mid-forties, rise consistently over a longer period of thirty years until the

[1] All British balance of payments estimates are taken from Imlah, *Economic Elements*. Imlah utilizes the same techniques employed by North and Simon in estimating nineteenth-century net capital flows. However, it should be noted that Imlah's transportation account, which is an important part of his balance of payments, has been the subject of criticism. See particularly the article by Douglass C. North and Alan Heston, 'The Estimation of Shipping Earnings in Historical Studies of the Balance of Payments', *Canadian Journal of Economics and Political Science*, XXVI, No. 2 (May 1960), 265–76.

The sources of the British data which are used in the charts are primarily from Imlah, *Economic Elements*, pp. 94–8; I have removed trends or calculated rates of change (those series which result from such adjustment are available upon request). The index of home investment and imported foodstuffs on Chart 1 is from Thomas, *Migration and Economic Growth*, pp. 297 and 328 respectively. In Chart 2, exports of finished iron and steel goods are also from Thomas, *Migration and Economic Growth*, p. 293.

mid-1870s, fall to a secular trough in the mid-1890s and then expand until the First World War. Not surprisingly, this configuration is very much like the general movement of import prices. (See Charts 1 and 2.) Even if we examine growth rates in imports in current prices, there is absolutely no evidence of Kuznets cycles which might be identified with hypothesized British income-output movements.

At first sight, the lack of evidence of long swings in imports in current prices, even after trend removal, would seem to support the implied position of many current students of British economic history that the interaction of home and foreign investment eliminated Kuznets cycles in aggregate income and output. After further study, however, this conclusion does not seem justified.

When we deflate import values by import prices, deflated imports do indeed reveal long swings after 1860, while the movements prior to 1860 are questionable (Chart 1). It is not a violent fluctuation even in the trendless index, but this is precisely what we hypothesized, given the inverse relationship between home and foreign investment and the resulting relative stability in aggregate demand over the long swing. So mild are the fluctuations in income that movements in real import demand over the long swing are completely smothered by raw material and agricultural foodstuff price movements.[1]

Are British deflated import movements positively correlated with income? Assuming a positive correlation between income growth (or some relevant component of income which exhibits long swings, such as consumption) and the rate of domestic investment, we can make some meaningful tests.[2] Cairncross's

---

[1] One cannot explain the evidence of long swings in deflated British imports by terms of trade movements. Imlah's net barter terms of trade *do* reveal long swings positively correlated with domestic investment and with deflated imports. However, these long swings in the net barter terms of trade occur with even more violent amplitude prior to the 1850s, while deflated imports reveal long swings only *after* the 1850s.

[2] After this paper was submitted, Feinstein's estimates of British domestic investment and net national income appeared in the *Economic Journal*. Regretfully, his estimates did not appear soon enough for me to make use of them in this study. C. H. Feinstein, 'Income and Investment in the United Kingdom, 1856–1914', *Economic Journal*, LXXI, No. 282 (June 1961), 367–85.

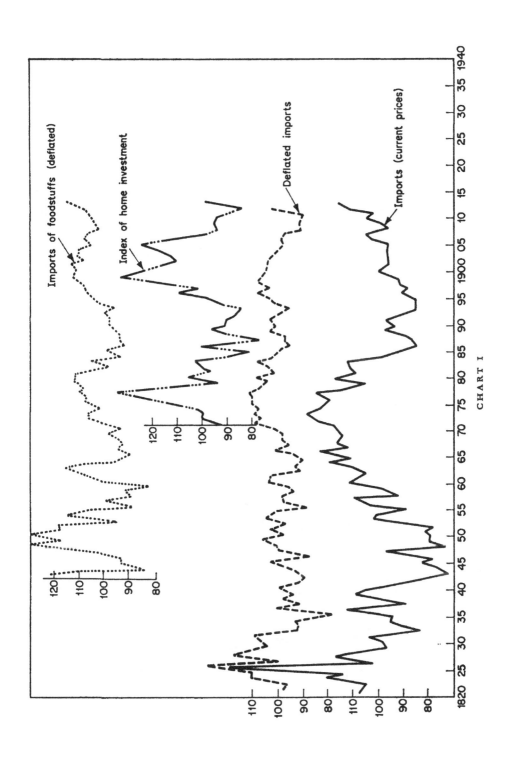

CHART I

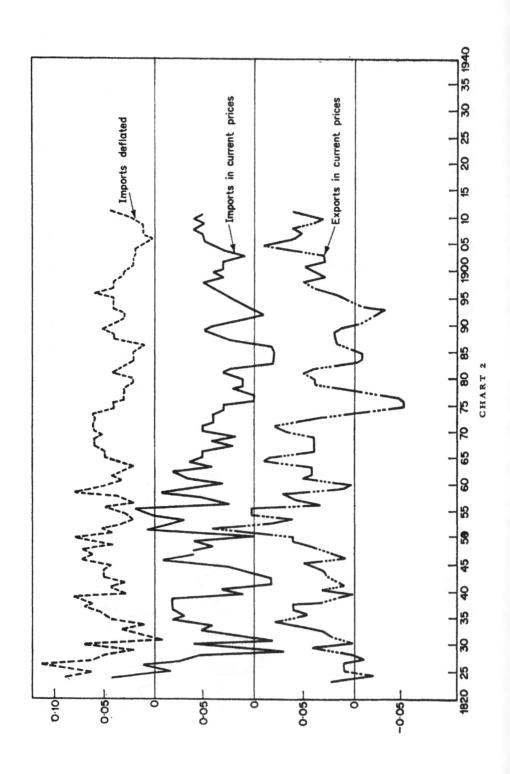

Imports deflated

Imports in current prices

Exports in current prices

CHART 2

series of British home investment from 1871–1913 is available, and has been used. Both the home investment and deflated imports series were used after removing their trends and smoothing. A simple univariate regression exhibits a positive correlation between the two series, where the explanatory power of domestic investment (I^{uk}) over deflated imports (M_D) is surprisingly high:

$$[1871–1913]\ M_D = 73.47 + 0.2597\ I^{uk} \quad R^2 = 0.837$$
$$(0.0190) \qquad R = 0.915,$$

and as we might have expected, the coefficient of I^{uk} is low, 0.26, reflecting the relative mildness of income movements compared with domestic investment.

The tentative conclusion is that not only were there long swings in deflated imports but that they were positively related to 'income' movements, although mild enough to be eliminated by active, and inversely correlated, import price movements. When deflated imports were at high levels in the late 1840s and early 1850s, import prices reached a secular trough; when deflated imports troughed in the mid-1860s, prices achieved fantastic heights; and finally, when deflated imports peaked in the mid-late 1890s, prices again fell to a secular trough. Although general world price movements were little different from British import price movements, the violence in amplitude of those prices must surely be partially explained by supply conditions in the American cotton and grain markets prior to 1870/80. Thus, it is the variation from the general world price trend in agricultural and raw material prices which removes the evidence of long swings in British import demand. For approximately two decades, the 1860s and 1870s, American wheat exports played an extremely important role in dictating the state of the grain market, while prior to 1860 the cotton market was almost entirely dominated by American exports. Both these commodities make up by far the largest share of British imports.

One more observation might be made before discussing the more violent swings in export movements. Deflated imports reveal Kuznets cycles after the late 1850s and until 1913, but the evidence of long swings *before* the American Civil War is thin indeed. This lack of long swings in British history prior to the 1850s is also true of net capital exports, which had configurations closer to seven to ten-year cycles than to twenty-year cycles, and of merchandise exports, which did not reveal long swings until the late 1840s and early 1850s. Was the same thing true of British income movements?

Since net capital exports were certainly no more severe in their amplitude and were less important as a share in total investment prior to the 1860s,[1] any explanation for observed stability in income-output movements should be attributable to the pattern of British home investment itself. In this respect, Thomas disagrees with Lewis and O'Leary, since he believes that there is no evidence of British building cycles from 1830–50.[2] Cooney, in a recent article, puts the argument in even stronger terms: 'The first main point to be made here is that there does not seem to be enough evidence to establish the existence of a (roughly) twenty-year building cycle in British history before 1870.'[3] Cairncross and Weber also support the view that, prior to 1850 at least, there is evidence of inherent seven- to ten-year cycles but none of building cycles.[4] Based mainly on Shannon's brick index,[5] Cairncross and Weber date major peaks in 1819, 1825, 1836, and 1847, and major troughs in 1821, 1832, and 1842.

Over the Kuznets cycle the movements in British exports were much more apparent than in imports. Generally, the rate of expansion in British exports was inversely related to deflated imports (and thus, presumably, to income), and exhibited more violent amplitude; this is true in both rates of change (Chart 2) and in the trendless series (Chart 3).

Deflated exports, as percentage deviations about a trend,

[1] Matthews, *The Business Cycle*, p. 222.

[2] Thomas, *Migration and Economic Growth*, p. 175.

[3] Cooney, 'Long Waves in Building in the British Economy of the Nineteenth Century', p. 258.

[4] A. K. Cairncross and B. Weber, 'Fluctuations in Building in Great Britain, 1785–1849', *The Economic History Review*, Second Series, IX, No. 2 (December 1956), 283–97.

[5] H. A. Shannon, 'Brick – a trade index', *Economica*, New Series, No. 1 (1934), pp. 300–18.

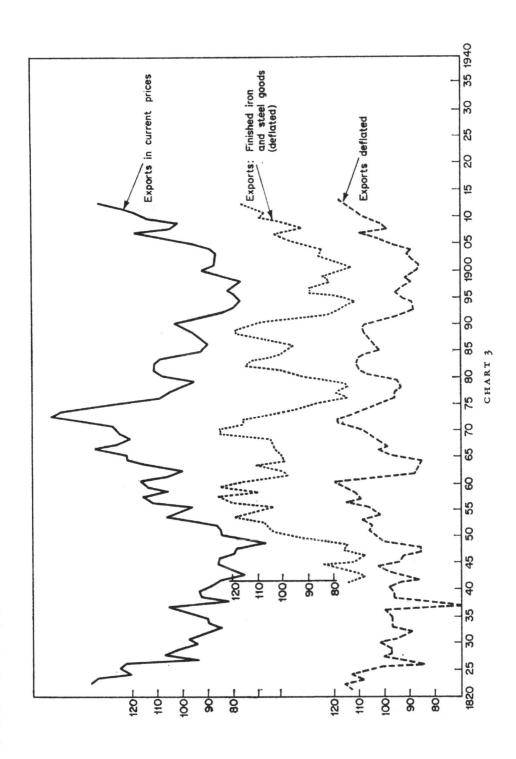

CHART 3

exhibit almost four long swings. The first rose from low levels in the 1840s to increasingly higher rates of export in the late 1850s and terminated with a trough in the early mid-1860s. The next long swing rose to a peak in the early 1870s and fell to a trough late in the 1870s. The third rose to a double peak in the early and late 1880s with an intermediate trough, and then fell to a trough at the turn of the century. Exports, then, expanded continually up to 1913 and the war. These long swings are less evident in the trendless current price series, but they are quite clear in rates of change.

The dating for deflated exports and imports with their trends removed is given in Table II. After 1870, the inverse correlation between export and import movements is quite striking, with imports generally leading by from one to three years. Prior to 1870 the inverse relationship almost disappears, while before 1860, of course, there is not enough evidence of a long swing in imports to date them. The inverse relationship between imports and exports seems to have become more consistent and precise as the century progressed. Can we go one step farther and suggest that the same would also hold true of net capital exports and the rate of home investment?

Deflated British exports moved inversely with deflated British imports, at least over most of the latter half of the nineteenth century, but they also moved *directly* with United States import fluctuations. This was true for the period after the later 1840s and until 1913, but there was no long swing in deflated British exports from 1820–50. (There *was* a long swing in the rates of growth of exports in current prices over the nineteenth century as a whole, including 1820–50. This is discussed below.) Table II compares the dating of deflated British exports and deflated American imports. Although there is obvious similarity in movement and timing throughout – but not in amplitude, the lead-lag relationship is much better in the latter half of the nineteenth century. Indeed, the timing of the British and American series is so close after 1860, especially for a comparison of annual data, as to suggest that American import demand may have played an important role in determining the rate of expansion of total British exports.

Fortunately we can apply a better test than this to determine the importance of the American market in conditioning the state of the British export industry. Increments in total British exports to foreign countries and British exports to the United States can be compared – the data are available in the British *Parliamentary Papers*. Were Kuznets cycles in the rate of expansion of British exports in current prices caused by violent

TABLE II*

	(1) U.S. Deflated Imports (trendless *and* annual)	(2) British-Deflated Exports (trendless *and* annual)		(3) British Deflated Imports (trendless *and* annual)
Trough	1821			
Peak	1836			
Trough	1843	1848		
Peak	1854	1860		
Trough	1862	1864		
Peak	1872	1871	Trough	1864
Trough	1878	1878	Peak	1877
Peak	1883	1882	Trough	—
Trough	[1885]	[1885]	Peak	—
Peak	[1888]	[1889]	Trough	1886
Trough	1898	1901	Peak	1898
Peak	1913T	1913T	Trough	1910

* Where T means last year in series.

fluctuations in American demand? The average share of total British exports going to America is significant: the highest occurred between the decades of the 1880s and 1890s, when approximately 20 per cent of British exports to foreign nations went to the United States. The marginal share, the ratio of first differences, was much higher, reaching its peak in the 1890s when 45 per cent of changes in British exports was attributable to changes in exports to the United States. The decade averages are given in Table III.

Even more impressive is the striking similarity between the movements of first differences in total British exports and exports to America shown in Chart 4. From 1850–1900 these series move together both in the smoothed and annual data. In the decade and a half after 1900 the series exhibit much less similarity, when American markets apparently ceased to play as vital a role for British export industry over the long swing. It should be clear, however, that fluctuations in American demand must have been a major cause for long swings in the rate of expansion of the British export industry 1850–1900.

In the 1830s and 1840s, although there is no evidence of a long swing in deflated British exports, the data on current exports in rates of change do reveal a long swing positively related to movements in American imports. In rates of change, British exports fell to a trough in 1824, reached a peak in 1834 and fell to a trough in 1839. United States imports, in rates of change, rose from a trough in the 1820s to a peak in 1833 and fell to a trough in 1842. Averaged over the period 1833–42 as a whole, the value of British exports to the United States constituted only 15 per cent of the total value of British exports. The *proportional* fluctuations, as in the period 1860–1900, were much greater. The average ratio of changes in exports to the United States to changes in total British exports was as high as 58 per cent. There is only one year between 1833–42 when the series move in opposite directions.

Matthews concludes from this evidence that 'the state of the American market was therefore the most important single factor in bringing prosperity or depression to British export industries.'[1] There are two problems, however, about such a strong conclusion concerning the effect of American import demand on English industry during the 1830s and 1840s. First, American imports in current prices *and* deflated exhibited long swings. Why were British exports affected only in current prices? This was not true of later years. Second, the fluctuation in British exports in current prices was extremely mild even in rates of change, and certainly nothing like those which appeared after the 1860s. It is thus difficult to believe that American import demands seriously imposed long swing fluctuations on the British export industry at this stage of the nineteenth century, and certainly there is no evidence that the British economy as a whole was enmeshed in the long swing mechanism. It seems more likely that the direct effects of the American

[1] R. C. O. Matthews, *A Study in Trade Cycle History: 1833–1842* (Cambridge: The University Press, 1954), pp. 43–4.

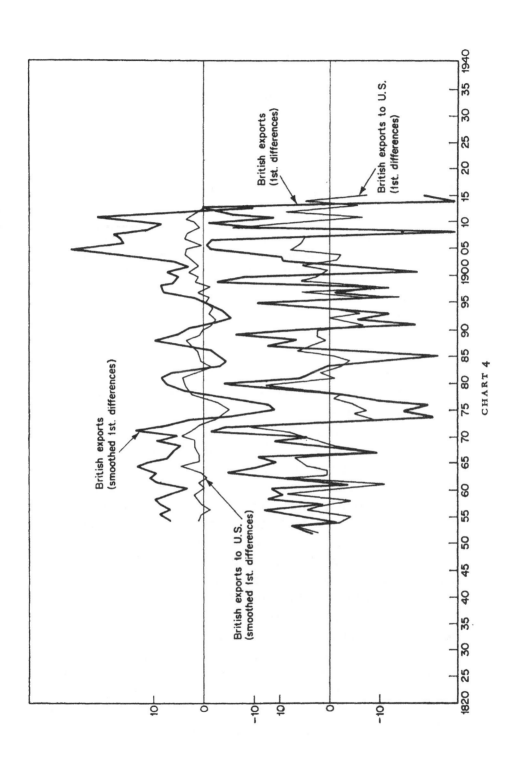

CHART 4

long swing on British development began during the period 1848–64 when evidence of Kuznets cycles in British exports became clear (although the British domestic economy at this stage was not yet undergoing long swings).

There is another interesting aspect of this comparison. Prior to and after 1870, when both series expanded rapidly, increases in British exports exceeded increases in exports to the United States. This is to be expected over a long period where secular expansion of the export industry was not dependent upon

TABLE III

	British exports to U.S. ÷ total British exports	Net change in British exports to U.S. ÷ net changes in total British exports
1850–9	0·19	0·14
1860–9	0·13	0·17
1870–9	0·14	0·39
1880–9	0·18	0·38
1890–9	0·19	0·45
1900–9	0·16	0·18
1910–13	0·16	0·20

United States demand alone. It is also true that changing American factor proportions must have caused a proportional shift out of British exports over time. But things are quite different at troughs of long swings. Prior to 1870 and in periods of depression in the American market, total British exports decreased at a lesser rate than did American imports from Great Britain, while after 1870 changes in total British exports moved more violently during *both* booms and prolonged depressions over the Kuznets cycle. This suggests that prior to 1870 only the United States was undergoing long swings in demand for British products, while after 1870 other developing nations with demands for British manufactures must also have been undergoing long swings similar in timing to American movements. This conclusion seems consistent with earlier movements as well, since Matthews' figures show consistently lower negative first differences in total British exports than in British exports to the United States during American depressions from 1833–42. I will return to this point below in the discussion of British capital exports.

In summary, it appears that long swings in United States development had an immediate effect upon British conditions through British export movements and, to a much lesser extent, via British import prices.

The similarities begin with balance of trade movements. Just as with American trade balance movements, the British trade balance deficit grew progressively worse during periods of domestic boom, becoming less unfavourable during periods of domestic depression and massive capital export. After 1860, American trade balance fluctuations inversely related to domestic long swings were almost entirely due to violent income, and thus import, movements. British trade balance fluctuations were certainly less violent, but their significant amplitude was due entirely to fluctuations in the rate of export expansion, since imports in current prices reveal no long swing. Thus, improvement in the British trade balance during depressions in domestic investment is not normally to be explained by a reduction in import values (although real import demand decreased) but rather by an expansion of export values.

Long swings in the British balance of trade really did not begin until 1860. However, choosing a somewhat arbitrary date of 1847, the trade balance exhibited a mild secular improvement from the large deficit of 1847 up to 1859; became sharply unfavourable from 1859 to the early mid-1860s, but remained constant and finally improved gradually up to 1872. From 1872 to the late 1870s, the trade balance was progressively unfavourable until 1886; from 1886 until 1902, it again deteriorated cumulatively, at which point it again improved until about 1911 (see Chart 5). Severe movements resembling long swings did not begin in the trade balance, then, until the late 1850s, which were also the initiating years of the more violent long swings in exports.[1] The dating of deflated exports, the trade

[1] Although rates of growth of imports in current prices do not reveal long swings over the nineteenth century as a whole, and deflated imports do not reveal long swings prior to the 1850s, the period 1828–41 *does* exhibit a movement in import values (in rates of change) similar to export movements. Indeed, this is the *only* period when import values indicate evidence of something akin to the long swing mechanism. Apparently, although real income movements do not seem to reveal a long swing 1820–40 and thus similarly for deflated imports, price

balance, deflated imports and domestic investment is given in
Table IV. I should point out that imports in current prices do
not exhibit long swings, but deflated values are included only
as an approximation of hypothesized 'income' movements.

TABLE IV*

	Inverted British Trade Balance Deficit (annual data)	Net Export of British Capital (annual data)	Deflated Exports (trendless)		Home Investment (trendless)	Deflated Imports (trendless)
Trough	1847(?)		1848			
Peak	1859	1859	1860			
Trough	1868	1862	1864			
Peak	1872	1872	1871	Trough	1871	1864
Trough	1877	1877	1878	Peak	1877	1877
Peak	—	—	1882	Trough	—	—
Trough	—	—	[1885]	Peak	—	—
Peak	1886	1890	[1889]	Trough	1887	1886
Trough	1902	1898	1901	Peak	1899	1898
Peak	1911	1913T	1913T	Trough	1912	1910

* Where T means last year in series.
Source: The home investment series was taken from Thomas, *Migration and Economic Growth*
Table 100, p. 290.

In the British balance of payments, just as in American
experience, the most obvious evidence of Kuznets cycles is in
the flow of capital. The timing of net capital exports was similar
to export and trade balance movements, but the amplitude of
capital flows was more violent – though not as violent as
American net capital imports. After 1870, net capital exports
and home investment did indeed complement each other in a
consistent fashion. Nevertheless, there is no evidence of long
swings in the rate of capital export prior to the late 1850s and
early 1860s; after that time the amplitudes of these long swings
in capital flows unquestionably became more severe. Prior to

fluctuations (primarily American cotton prices) are severe enough to cause a
movement in import values similar to, and exceeding in rate of change, export
movements. Thus, in spite of the long swing in rates of change of exports in
current values from 1824–39, the trade balance does not reflect it in such a way
as to extend the evidence of long swings in the trade balance (positively related
to export movements) back before the 1850s. Compared to other nineteenth-
century movements this is a very unusual period in English history indeed. One
cannot help but be further impressed with the dissimilarity between British
movements prior to the 1850s and afterwards. Apparently the long swing,
which was already so evident in United States development, either had not yet
foisted itself upon English development or whatever endogenous conditions
were necessary to generate the long swing were not yet in evidence. Surely the
popularized mechanism of the interaction of the Atlantic economy was not the
same prior to the 1850s as after those years.

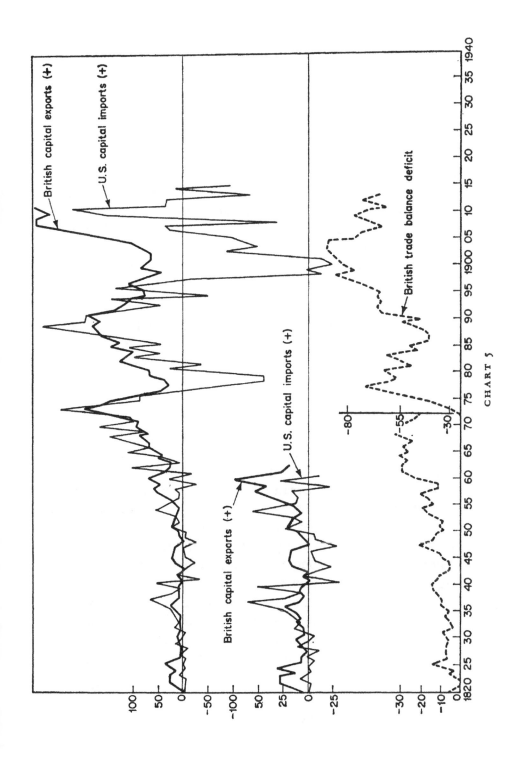

CHART 5

the late 1850s, net capital exports from Great Britain played a much smaller role in British development and as a share in total investment. It is also true that prior to the late 1850s any fluctuations in net capital exports seem to have been primarily of the seven- to ten-year variety, peaking in 1835, 1844, 1850, and 1859, troughing in 1840, 1847, and 1853. At least from 1830–45, net capital exports moved consistently with building indices;[1] nor is this positive relation inconsistent with experience after 1870, when domestic and foreign investment moved inversely over the long swing, for in that period as well domestic and foreign investment moved positively over *short* cycles.[2]

From a peak outflow of capital in 1859, net capital exports fell to a trough in 1862. The first complete swing rose from there to an extremely high level of capital outflow in 1872 and then fell to a severe trough in 1877. This long swing rose rather gradually to the end of the 1860s before the massive outflow, peaking in 1872. The second secular swing rose from a trough in 1877 to a peak in 1890, then fell into the prolonged depression of the 1890s – 1898 being the poorest year. From the decade of the 1890s, capital exports continued to increase until 1913, quite sharply from 1905 to the war (see Chart 5).

The net export of British capital, therefore, is positively correlated with the export of goods, and negatively correlated with the trade balance deficit, home investment, and deflated imports. On average, net capital exports lead deflated exports by about two years (the lead would possibly be longer if export movements were expressed in annual data). And we find home investment (inverted) leading net capital exports by one or two years. Consequently, foreign and domestic investment do not quite mesh over the long swing: it may be quite true that this lag of British savers moving out of domestic and into foreign investment explains the apparent evidence of a Juglar cycle.

Although the evidence seems to support the hypothesis that American import demands played an extremely important role in determining the level and movements of British exports, at

[1] Cairncross and Weber, 'Fluctuations in Building in Great Britain, 1785–1849', p. 285.
[2] Cairncross, *Home and Foreign Investment.*

least after 1850, it is more difficult to make the same statement for capital flows. Surely the timing and general pattern of British exports and American imports of capital were extremely similar. Nevertheless, it is difficult to say much more than this for the nineteenth century as a whole. Prior to the late 1850s, there was no long swing in the rate of British capital exports and yet there was in American capital imports. After the 1850s, it is clear that American capital imports moved as if they dominated British capital exports due to the similarity of timing and patterns over the long swing, but could this be due to long swings in other countries as well? One bit of evidence which positively points to the importance of American demands for capital has its source in Madden's research.[1] His estimates show that from 60–5 per cent of the fluctuations in British capital exports from 1860–80 were due to fluctuations in American demands for capital over the long swing. If this were true of all the long swings in the nineteenth century we could conservatively conclude that American demands did indeed directly determine the extent and timing of British capital export fluctuations over the long swing.

If we discard the temptation to apply Madden's research to all the long swings in capital flows after the 1850s, then it would seem that it takes a combination of *three* things to cause a long swing in net capital movements in the case of a capital exporter. Long swings in the demand for capital in the United States were not enough to cause similar British movements (that is, pre-1850s) either because the United States was too small as a source of demand or, *and more likely*, one of the other two necessary ingredients was missing. If income growth was approximately constant in the rest of the world outside of the United States, it should have been relatively simple for British investors to shift between American securities and those of other countries according to the vitality of American develop-ment and the return on capital, as was apparently the case

[1] John J. Madden, *British Investment in the United States, 1860–1880*. Conference on Research in Income and Wealth, unpublished manuscript (September 1956), Table 10, p. 46. I would like to thank Professor Madden for allowing me to refer to his work.

before the 1850s. Thus, a long swing in American development and demands for foreign capital need not be reflected in total British capital exports as well: nor, for that matter, did long swings in British exports of goods (1848–64) have an *immediate* effect upon the pattern of growth of the British economy.

One of the missing ingredients may be the lack of similar and inverse movements in the pace of development of the lending country. If Great Britain were undergoing a long swing as well, surely one would also expect to find a long swing in the rate of British capital export. The problem then is why there is so little evidence of long swings in British internal development prior to the 1850s. Can we then suggest that American long swings in some indirect way triggered movements in Great Britain?[1] This supposition seems more likely than to attribute the creation of a domestic long swing mechanism in Great Britain to something purely endogenous to the British system. For why do British and American movements exhibit this curious and suspicious inverse relation, and why did British long swings come relatively late in the century after the United States had been undergoing them for some time?

The second ingredient, which seems to be in evidence only after 1870 and which may help explain the appearance of Kuznets cycles in British capital exports after 1860, is the possible new occurrence of long swings in the pace of growth in other newly developing, raw material- and foodstuff-producing nations. Not only did Canada, Australia, and Argentina, for example, exhibit what look like long swings in their consumption of foreign capital after 1870, but their movements were inversely related to British internal development as well. If, however, Madden's estimates quoted above are applicable to a large part of the period 1860–1913, then the importance of variation in demand for British capital in other countries, similar in timing to United States demands, seems very much reduced. For that matter, fluctuations in net capital imports into Canada, Australia, and Argentina may have been the effect, not the cause, of fluctuations in British capital exports.

[1] For an assertion of this intuitive feeling see Cooney, 'Long Waves in Building in the British Economy of the Nineteenth Century', p. 267.

This paper is not intended to examine exhaustively the possible direct interactions between British and American balance of payments, nor is it intended to determine and test the causes of British balance of payments fluctuations over the long swing. What I have attempted here is to leave open the door so ably set ajar by Brinley Thomas in his examination of the interactions in the development of the Atlantic economy. The general impression in this preliminary analysis is that the systematic relationship between British and American development, in the nature of a Kuznets cycle, had its source not in Great Britain but in the United States. If that statement is supported by future research, it is only a small step to imagine how the powerful inverse relation in Anglo-American development spilled over into other newly developing nations with factor endowments similar to those of the United States.

It seems clear that a large part of the Anglo-American interaction can be explained by the direct effects upon British export industry of fluctuating United States demands for imports. Nevertheless, this conclusion is not meant to depreciate the importance of labour migration as an explanation for the inverse pattern of growth between these two countries. Long swings in American demands for imports can be traced back at least as far as 1820, but migration of labour from Europe to America did not really attain impressive heights until the 1840s and 1850s; long swings in British development do not seem to be in evidence before that time, but very soon afterwards. However, we now have a second alternative hypothesis: from 1848–64 British exports (current *and* deflated) showed definite long swings, but net capital exports and home investment did not. Could these fluctuations in British exports reflect an initiation of the transfer of American long swings into British development via demands for British exports? It seems more likely, however, that the interaction was a result of both the demand for goods and for migrants: variations in American import demands strengthened the inverse movement, which became clear after the first really important flow of factors, notably labour, across the Atlantic.

4 Overseas Lending and Internal Fluctuations: 1870–1914

A. G. FORD

[This article was first published in *The Yorkshire Bulletin of Economic and Social Research*, Vol. 17, No. 1 (1965).]

The effects of the waves of British overseas lending before 1914 in converting certain empty underdeveloped countries into prospering and growing (primary producing) economies are commonplace, as is also the fact that their advance was uneven and marked with crises. What has received less attention is their influence on the British economy itself, and this paper seeks to examine some of these effects – in particular their short-run influence on fluctuations in British economic activity, although longer-run forces will be noted too. For Britain was not unscathed when a crisis broke abroad (occasioned perhaps by the variability of British overseas lending), since not only was she a *lending* economy, but also an *export* economy.

Estimates of the size of British overseas lending have been provided by A. H. Imlah,[1] who calculated the British current account balance of payments and adjusted this for gold movements to give a net 'capital export' figure for each year of the period. This gives us an *ex post* or realized figure which is of great importance in getting the facts right, but is unsatisfactory in terms of economic motivation since it is the resultant of various economic forces which have been set in motion by decisions to lend abroad (and, of less importance and usually neglected, by the decisions of others to lend to Britain). Rather, for our purposes, an *ex ante* estimate or indicator of overseas lending, a statistic reflecting the decision to lend (or borrow),

[1] A. H. Imlah, *Economic Elements in the Pax Britannica* (Harvard, 1958), pp. 72–5.

is required. This is provided least unsatisfactorily by the series of overseas issues on the London Stock Exchange,[1] which formed a principal vehicle of British overseas lending. It is comforting to find that both these estimates (although one is 'net' and the other is only partial) are of roughly the same magnitude and exhibit similar behaviour in long-run fluctuations,[2] but a distinct tendency for overseas issues to lead *ex post* estimates both in short-run fluctuations and in turning points. At times overseas issues amounted in size to almost 10 per cent of British net national income, and completely dwarfed the Bank of England's Reserve which rarely rose above £35–40 million. To modern eyes foreign lending on such a scale appears unthinkable, the more so when it was conducted under a strict gold standard. Here arises the first query: how did Britain transfer such sums abroad without straining her adherence to the gold standard? How in fact was a decision to lend abroad (represented by an overseas issue) translated into a subsequent balance of payments current account surplus (*ex post* capital export), for when issues were high, so was the surplus, and when issues were low, a low surplus prevailed, so far as underlying trends were concerned? Indeed, it will be argued that it was not so much the case that outward-looking Britain dutifully lent abroad an already emergent balance of payments currents account surplus, but that Britain's *ex ante* overseas lending and the use made of it tended to create the requisite surplus to finance it without straining the Reserve permanently. In investigating this with the use of some economic theory the analysis will provide clues not only to the mode of transfer but also to the likely repercussion effects on British home activity.

In considering a transfer of funds abroad it is essential to ask first, how the funds were raised in the lender, and second, how they were used by the borrower or recipient country. For on the answers to these, which fortunately can be arranged into

---

[1] C. Hobson, *The Export of Capital* (London, 1914), p. 219.

[2] See Chart 1, where by the use of nine years moving averages cyclical fluctuations are separated out from the raw figures, to leave what is arbitrarily designated as 'trend' values.

several convenient categories, will depend the ease or otherwise
of the transfer of the funds *and* the nature of the internal fluctuations to be expected as a consequence.

Funds might be raised in the lender at the expense of home
spending (for example, by substituting overseas lending for
lending to domestic industrialists whose investment spending
would then fall, or by lenders cutting their own consumption
spending to increase their savings which they employed in the
purchase of new issues of overseas securities) and this will be
designated case IA. Alternatively, they might be raised from
previously idle funds or from credit creation, designated case
IB. Initially a transfer of funds to overseas ownership, however
they were raised, would cause balance of payments strain,
involving perhaps the loss of gold. This strain would persist
in case IB but would be alleviated in case IA. For home
spending would decline, thus reducing incomes, output, and
employment in the lender so that its demand for imported
goods would decline. This fall in imports would tend to improve the current account of the lender's balance of payments
which could be set against the worsening capital account so
that balance of payments strain would be alleviated at the
expense of the creation of some home unemployment.

Recipients, or borrowers, of these funds might use them
merely to increase their holdings of gold and foreign exchange
(case IIA) with no immediate or direct influences on the lending
economy. Secondly, they might use them to buy extra imports
directly (case IIB): in a two-country world or a world in
which there existed strong trading connections between lender
and borrower this use would afford considerable help to the
lender. For the lender's export sales would rise, thereby offsetting (somewhat or even completely) the fall in home
spending which the raising of the funds had entailed (assuming
case IA). Hence the fall in output, employment, and imports of
the lending country would be diminished and the balance of
payments improvement on current account would come about
largely by a rise in exports rather than a fall in imports. If
coupled with IB, activity would rise in the lender as its exports
sales rose, and this stimulus would be transmitted to the

borrower as the lender bought more of the borrower's exports: in these circumstances the improvement in the lender's current account and the deterioration in the borrower's current account would each be less than where IIB was coupled with IA. Thirdly, they might be used to finance increased domestic spending in the borrowing country (either investment, consumption, or government spending) and this is designated case IIC. Here the borrower's spending and incomes would rise, bringing rising import purchases from the lender in a two-country world so that balance of payments strain would be alleviated for the lender as its exports rose and the emergent unemployment in the lender would be mitigated in case IA. In case IB the balance of payments strain would be alleviated for the lender likewise but to a smaller extent than in the former case, while expansionary forces would spread back from the lender to the borrower.

To these 'automatic' (i.e. occurring without changes in economic policies) effects must be added several other effects which would aid or impede the process of transfer. First, if the overseas lending bore fixed-interest charges payable immediately, these would tend to assist the position of the lender and impair the position of the borrower so far as balances of payments were concerned. Secondly, the movements of funds might cause in some cases prices in the borrowing country to rise *relatively* to prices in the lending country, and thereby facilitate the transfer of funds in a two-country world by helping to generate a bigger current account surplus for the lender, and a bigger deficit on current account for the borrower, than would have occurred under conditions of price stability. Thirdly, in a many-country world the increased imports of the borrower (cases IIB and IIC) would be spread over several countries and would not be concentrated on the lender's products, so that its exports would not rise so much. In case IA this would not involve much, if any, extra balance of payments strain for the lender as compared with the two-country world, only rather more unemployment would persist; in case IB there would be more balance of payments strain.

It is clear then that particular economic circumstances will

D

determine the extent to which the transfer of funds can be achieved automatically and the size of the resultant deficit for the lender which monetary (and fiscal) policies would have to handle, but it cannot be doubted that these 'automatic' effects will generally and predictably make for a lessening of strain, for the lender by cutting its initial deficit. Less predictable, however, are the effects of a surge in overseas lending on the lender's economic activity which is the main theme of this paper. Conceivably, an increase in overseas lending could lead to depression in the lender if we considered the coupling of IA and IIA in a two-country world or again IA and IIA *or* IIB *or* IIC in a many-country world. On the other hand a boom could occur, if balance of payments problems could be neglected, in the lender as well as in the borrower with the coupling of IB with IIC, for example, which would cause the lender's export sales to rise and thus to bring rising output and incomes. The specific circumstances are all-important here, and armed with these theoretical tools let us turn to the British position between 1870–1914.

It is clear from Chart 1 that when overseas investment was high, home investment was low, and *vice versa*, so far as long-term trends (nine-year moving averages) are concerned, although short-run deviations present a more variable picture. The precise theoretical mechanism to explain this alternation of 18–20-year cycles in British home and overseas investment is still the subject of speculation and controversy. Varying emphasis is laid on the 'pull' of overseas prospects attracting both capital and labour from Europe: the 'push' of poor home prospects of low interest rates, unemployment, and low real wages inducing the export of capital and labour; and the way in which such migrations help to cause, and are associated with, the inverse 18–20 cycles in British and American constructional activity, and the behaviour of the British terms of trade.[1]

[1] See for example, Brinley Thomas, *Migration and Economic Growth* (London, 1954); A. K. Cairncross, *Home and Foreign Investment* (Cambridge, 1958); D. J. Coppock, 'The Causes of Business Fluctuations', *Manchester Statistical Society*, 1959. This paper accepts the inverse long-run relationship and seeks nothing more ambitious than remarks on its consequences for British activity and international accounts.

To such orderly features may be added the chance factors which can prove so annoying for neat theoretical patterns but so important in economic history. For example, Argentina in the early 1880s enjoyed strong federal government and had put down the Indians of the interior so that it became a feasible – and profitable – proposition to build railways to open up the Pampas. British investors' imagination was caught, yields offered were high, and a tremendous surge of overseas investment was directed to this area on a greater scale than could be absorbed into real capital formation. Disquieting tales from Buenos Aires led to disillusionment, the drying-up of loans in 1889, and the crash of 1890, as immediate prospects waned with the short time-horizon of some British lenders. Yet railways were built, agricultural output and export volumes expanded sharply after 1893 to be enhanced by rising prices after 1896 so that by the turn of the century Argentina could meet her previously defaulted overseas debt-service commitments, pay rising dividends, and thus return to favour with British lenders. By 1904 London new issues for Argentina were rising fast to reach a peak in 1911, just over 20 years after the earlier peak in 1889. It may not be too fanciful to suggest a different form of cycle based on excesses of enthusiasm and revulsion among lenders and on the simple fact that projects such as railways take *time* to construct and to develop traffic on a profitable scale as land has to be cleared, prepared, sown before any crops can be moved to ports for export. A period of upsurge in overseas investment to a favoured area on an excessive scale is followed by disillusion and crisis once it is realized that earlier judgements were excessively optimistic and short-sighted with no immediate returns accruing. In the period of revulsion by investors the borrowing country's projects are completed and mature, and with expanding output and exports any defaulted interest payments may be resumed, so that dividends on stock perhaps consigned to perdition as worthless are now paid on a rising scale. Memories are short and the country concerned is restored to favour gradually so that a new upsurge in borrowing may take place, the time involved being of the order of 15–20 years.

However, events in one country must not be viewed in isolation, for it was vitally important that fresh overseas issues should encounter a receptive market in London and not find that British savings were being claimed by domestic ventures. Hence, such a long cycle based on Argentine experience must be integrated with, and was indeed shaped by, the earlier factors of migration and building on each side of the Atlantic which could influence the prospects of Argentine new issues being taken up when offered in London. Furthermore, it may be recalled that Australia was a favourite destination for British funds in the 1880s but not in the 1900s when its place was taken by Canada, so that additional 'chance' factors may render such a loose 'Argentine-type' cycle inoperative.

One firm conclusion, however, does emerge from this long-run alternation of home and overseas investment: as a basic pattern it is appropriate to use case IA – funds for overseas lending raised at the expense of home expenditure – in analysing the effects of British overseas lending on her balance of payments and domestic activity and employment. Furthermore, from general knowledge of the character of much of British overseas lending and the principal areas to which it was directed, it is reasonable to conclude that the borrowing countries used the funds thus received to buy directly extra imports (case IIB) or to increase home expenditure as a result of which their import purchases expanded (case IIC). In a world in which there were strong trading ties between Britain and the underdeveloped borrowers, British exports would thus increase as a result of bilateral purchases, and perhaps as a result of multilateral forces as increased purchases by borrowers from other countries raised their incomes and hence the latter's purchases of British exports.

In Chart 1 the similarity in broad movements of overseas issues, the balance of trade, the ratio of exports to imports and overseas investment (*ex post*) is most striking. In periods of active foreign lending, as indicated by overseas issues, it is clear that export values rose relatively to import values, thereby lessening the adverse balance of trade (as compared with years of low overseas issues) and helping to bring about the increased balance of payments surplus on current account, necessary if capital exports calculated from balance of payments estimates are to show similar movements to overseas issues. Furthermore, when issues declined, the ratio of exports to imports declined, thereby bringing a worsening in the balance of trade and causing the current account surplus to decline. Crudely, three quarters of the excess of capital exports in periods of high

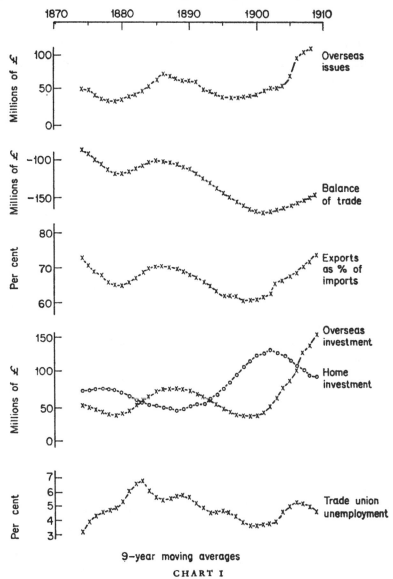

9–year moving averages

CHART I

lending over that prevailing in periods of low lending was attributable to such movements in these merchandise items.[1]

The earlier analysis allows us to explain these similar movements as follows. Rising overseas issues (the main vehicle of capital export) served to stimulate directly and indirectly British exports (both visible and invisible, including income from abroad), and the subsequent (multiplier) increases in home incomes and in imports were mitigated, or even more than offset, by the depressive influences from the falling trend behaviour of home investment (at whose expense the overseas lending had taken place) so that an increased current account surplus was generated to bring about the real transfer of capital abroad. With a long-term switch to home investment and away from overseas issues, exports stagnated (or even declined somewhat), while incomes and imports rose because the increased home investment was not offset by falling exports, so that the balance of payments current account surplus lessened, reflecting lower overseas investment. In this way the waves of overseas lending were transferred with little basic strain to the British balance of payments and the maintenance of specie payments.

But what of the long-run influences of these alternations of home and overseas investment on British economic activity and employment? To try to assess this, the long-term trend of Trade Union unemployment has been calculated although it must be remembered that this is only an indicator of the behaviour of employment in Britain and was of course subject to other forces than the above alternation – for example, the general level of world activity and its influence on British exports, or the British propensity to consume. Theoretical expectation is that unless increased export sales offset the decline in home spending as overseas lending rose unemployment would tend to increase in the conjuncture of case IA/IIB and IIC; or, in dynamic terms, if with rising overseas investment export sales growth did not accelerate sufficiently to offset the decline in home investment and so maintain the growth in

[1] See A. G. Ford, 'The Transfer of British Foreign Lending, 1870–1913' *Economic History Review*, Second Series, Vol. XI (December 1958), p. 304.

effective demand at a sufficient rate to absorb the growth in British productive capacity, the unemployment percentage might be expected to be greater than in periods of rising home investment, and *vice versa*. Indeed, it might be expected in an environment of multilateral trade and untied loans (despite the strong trading ties and Britain's role as a major industrial supplier) that £100 devoted to overseas investment would raise British exports (visible and invisible), and hence effective demand initially, by rather less than that sum,[1] while if devoted to home investment would increase effective demand by £100 in the first stage. On a long-term basis, then, one might expect unemployment to be rising as overseas investment rose, and to be falling as home investment rose.

In Chart 1 the nine-year moving average of Trade Union unemployment may be compared with the trends of home and overseas investment. The first feature is that the former curve is not so smooth in its wave-like motion as the latter two, nor secondly are the degrees of direct or inverse relationships so marked. In more detail as overseas investment declined from 1874 to 1879 unemployment rose; with the revival in overseas investment from 1879 to a trend peak in 1888 unemployment continued to rise until the middle 1880s after which it declined. The steady decline in overseas investment and the marked rise in home investment from 1888 to 1900 was associated with a steady decline in the unemployment trend from 5½ per cent to 3½ per cent roughly. After 1900 the revival in the overseas investment trend and the decline in the home investment trend were accompanied by a broadly rising tendency of the un-employment trend. Although it is realized that the unemploy-ment trend is an imperfect indicator of British activity and that it was subject to many other influences than the alternation of home and overseas investment in the *particular* economic environment, which has shaped the assumptions made, nevertheless the accord with theoretical expectation based on these plausible assumptions is too strong to be dismissed entirely. It would seem reasonable to conclude that variations in the trend of British overseas investment provided one

[1] Borrowers would spend some of the proceeds on non-British goods.

important factor influencing the trend of home employment; trend rises in overseas investment being related to trend rises in home unemployment, and *vice versa*.

Let us now turn away from longer-run influences and consider the relationships of deviations from trends – short-run

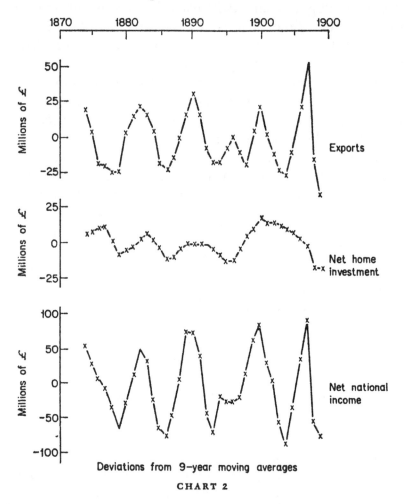

Deviations from 9–year moving averages

CHART 2

cycles or trade cycles – to assess any influences of British overseas investment on home fluctuations. In Chart 2 are presented movements in British export values, net home investment, net money national income, from which it is abundantly clear that *immediate* cause of fluctuations in British money incomes was fluctuations in merchandise export values,[1] aided or impeded by fluctuations in home investment. In more detail the fall in incomes to the trough of 1879 closely agreed with the decline in exports despite the rise in home investment to 1877, thereafter the collapse in home investment aggravated the slump. Rising exports and investment provided the main stimulus in the subsequent recovery with both exports and incomes attaining their peaks in 1882 and slumping afterwards to 1886, while domestic investment attained its peak in 1883. The main reason for the peak of incomes and employment in 1890 was provided by rising exports with small movements in home investment, thereafter the fall in exports brought the slump of 1893.[2] The influences of the limited recovery in exports on income after 1893 until 1896 were offset by the opposite behaviour of investment, and *vice versa* between 1896 and 1898, after which both moved together to bring the peak of 1900. After 1900 home investment declined steadily to 1908, thus aggravating the influence of declining exports on incomes until 1904, but only mitigating the effects of rapidly rising exports between 1904 and 1907 on employment and incomes, while both variables contributed to the slump of incomes after 1907 to 1909.

'In short, there emerges a strong positive correlation between fluctuations in exports on the one hand, and incomes and employment on the other, while it is clear that fluctuations in home investment show no such strong accord. Furthermore, the amplitude of the absolute fluctuations in export values was consistently 2 to $2\frac{1}{2}$ times as great as that of home investment, so that the former contributed more to 'multiplier' influences on incomes and was able to outweigh any dissimilar behaviour of investment.'[3]

[1] For simplicity merchandise exports have been depicted in the diagrams. If invisibles were to be incorporated, they would reinforce the cyclical movements of exports and the argument in the text may be taken to refer to exports (visible and invisible) equally as well as to visible exports alone.

[2] Unemployment is not plotted in chart 2, but has similar fluctuations to incomes.

[3] A. G. Ford, 'Notes on the Role of Exports in British Economic Fluctuations, 1870–1914', *Economic History Review*, Second Series, Vol. XVI (December 1963), p. 332.

These fluctuations in export values were the joint product of similar movements in prices and volumes, while the geographical break-down of exports provides varied behaviour of component series, with Europe providing the dominant source of fluctuations in total export values and showing the closest accord with cyclical turning-points in Britain. Indeed, the role of the 'Atlantic' economy in generating economic fluctuations in Britain needs re-examining in the light of the great proximate influence of the 'European' economy on British exports and activity.[1]

Such are the facts about British trade cycles. What, then, caused these fluctuations in exports? Our earlier analysis would suggest that *one* influence would be fluctuations in *ex ante* British overseas lending, for which overseas issues provide our indicator. A rise in issues, when used by the overseas borrowers, might be expected to be followed by a rise in British exports either directly or indirectly, as argued earlier, but with some time-lag, and likewise a fall in overseas issues, whether because a rise in Bank Rate made the flotation of loans a more costly business or because interest in an area had waned and mistrust arisen among British lenders, might be expected to bring in its wake a decline in British exports, unless swamped by such other factors as the general state of world activity. Whether such changes in exports brought positively associated changes in incomes would depend on the extent to which the issues were taken up at the expense of home spending: if wholly at the expense of home spending (IA), then in this particular economic environment British incomes would tend to sag; if from idle holdings (IB), then British incomes and imports might be expected to rise and to present balance of payments problems as the change in the current account surplus was inadequate to finance the outflow of capital. Hence the influence of overseas issue deviations on home activity depends not only on the use made of them and the sensitivity of British exports to them, but also on the way in which these issues were financed. (All this is in terms of deviations from trends and their behaviour.)

[1] A. G. Ford, op. cit., pp. 332–5.

In Chart 3 deviations of British overseas new issues from nine-year moving averages are presented together with deviations in total exports and in the 'value of world trade' index. Although British exports deviations and world trade deviations exhibited broadly similar cyclical behaviour (as

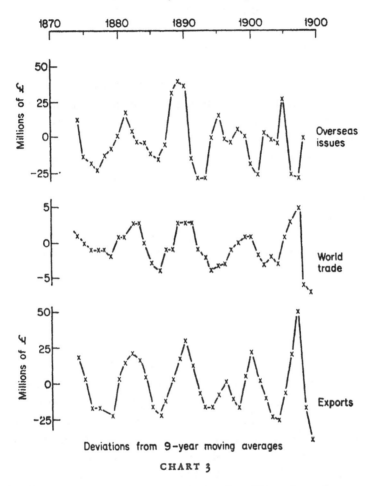

Deviations from 9-year moving averages

CHART 3

might be expected since British trade claimed an important share of world trade), it is of great interest that deviations in overseas issues exhibited a marked cyclical pattern but *led* fluctuations in exports and in world trade by one to two years. In addition, the amplitude in absolute terms of these (cyclical) movements in overseas issues was only a little less than that of exports.

As fluctuations in exports have been adduced as the main immediate cause of cyclical fluctuations in British incomes and employment, it is tempting to consider from the above evidence that these latter fluctuations were a direct result of changes in *ex ante* overseas lending by Britain. However, although there is some truth in this view, it is too simple and mechanical. The breakdown of changes in total exports into geographical areas makes it clear that the influence of variations in overseas issues on exports was *partially* bilateral, since in this period Britain lent very little to Europe which on the other hand provided a considerable part (on average at least two-fifths) of the explanation of absolute fluctuations in British export values.

Besides invoking these multilateral trading relations, it is necessary to take account of other less direct but important connections between British overseas lending and exports. First, extra finance was often a pre-condition of a rise in economic activity in various parts of the world (especially in those which adhered to some form of gold standard), which increased overseas lending by Britain helped to supply at least in the short-run, while the drying-up of overseas investment by Britain could impose a severe liquidity crisis, as well as deflationary pressures, in borrowing countries initially, which might easily spread to more developed monetary centres. Depressive tendencies could easily be initiated by the spread of declining expenditure and through the collapse of excessively optimistic expectations, just as expansionary forces were spread in the upswing. Secondly, rising or falling activity, initiated by the variability of British overseas lending, could touch off further expansionary forces elsewhere, not only through direct changes in trade flows, but also through psychological effects which caused the parallel revision upwards or downwards of marginal efficiency of capital estimates elsewhere. These may help to explain the distinct tendencies towards cyclical parallelism in Britain, France, and Germany especially,[1] which reacted on each other's economies, while

---

[1] A comparison of the reference cycles of these three countries reveals that all three were in the same phase in 83·1 per cent of all months between 1879 and

money markets too moved together and were particularly
close at times of crisis, so that the pervasive nature of fluctuations and crises in Europe was enhanced.

Support for this broad line of argument is provided by the
lead of deviations in overseas issues over deviations in the
'world trade' index, which damps the otherwise interesting
argument that a third, unmentioned, factor (gold discoveries,
for example) influenced both overseas issues and the course of
world trade. For if the same force influenced both trade and
issues, they might be expected to move together and not exhibit
this lead, which would then be unexplained. Yet some portion
of the explanation of the sensitivity of changes in British
exports to changes in overseas issues may lie in more random
factors – that one or another of the main trading countries
happened to be in the grip of a domestic investment cycle at
the appropriate times, which was reinforced by the earlier-
mentioned psychological forces.

Caution is, indeed, needed in interpreting the role of overseas issues and careful study of particular crises and cycles is
essential. A few casual remarks may suffice by way of illus-
tration. Although the decline in overseas issues from 1905 to
1907 was one influence in the subsequent decline in British
exports from 1907 to 1909, it was overshadowed by the
influence of the American financial troubles of 1906 and 1907
and their transmission to Europe via trading flows, psychological repercussions on expectations and monetary stringencies.
These troubles imposed the need for higher Bank Rate in
London in 1906 and 1907, which besides its effects on short-
term capital flows, served to check overseas issues in London
by increasing their costs and risks of failure, while they recovered sharply in 1908 when monetary stringency had eased,
and helped the recovery of British exports after 1909. Here
confidence in the main borrowing areas had remained high
despite the American troubles, for the crisis had not been
located in any of these areas – quite distinct from the position

---

1914, while the addition of the United States causes this to drop to 53·5 per cent
for all four countries. O. Morgenstern, *International Financial Transactions and
Business Cycles* (Princeton, 1959), p. 43.

in the 1890 crisis. In this episode an excessive surge of British lending to Argentina was reversed equally sharply in 1889 following disquieting reports and events in Buenos Aires. This cessation of lending brought an acute crisis in Argentina which reacted on London and on Barings in particular, besides spreading to European money markets; reappraisals of other overseas projects followed, business confidence was shaken, while the decline in issues after 1889 was followed by falling exports after 1890, particularly those to Europe and to the areas which had been borrowing heavily. With the fall in Bank Rate after 1890 new overseas issues did not revive (in contrast to the 1907–8 experience), for here confidence in the borrowing areas had been shattered since the source of the crisis was held to have been in one of them.[1] Export recovery was limited in the 1890s and a spurt in home investment revived the British economy after 1895.

One problem remains. Earlier it was asserted that as a basic long-run pattern overseas investment took place at the expense of home spending, a consequence of which in the particular environment discussed was a tendency for the increase in exports as lending abroad rose to be less than the decline in home spending so that activity would tend to be damped down or at best remain unchanged. However, in the short run deviations in exports, home activity (as measured by money incomes and employment), and imports were closely associated in a positive way[2] – exports variations were held to be the main proximate determinant of the British trade cycle. It would seem that perhaps other influences caused exports to deviate by more than could be attributed to the deviations in lending abroad alone, but more importance should be attached to the view that in the short run a considerable part of *ex ante* overseas lending was financed from previously idle holdings (the IB case) so that exports rose by more than the initial fall in home

---

[1] For a more detailed treatment of each of these episodes, see A. G. Ford, 'Argentina and the Baring Crisis of 1890', *Oxford Economic Papers*, 8 (June 1956), and 'Bank Rate, the British Balance of Payments, and the Burdens of Adjustment, 1870–1914', *Oxford Economic Papers*, 16 (March 1964).

[2] Import deviations have not been plotted here. See A. G. Ford, *The Gold Standard 1880–1914: Britain and Argentina* (Oxford, 1962), Ch. IV.

spending (if any) and transmitted expansionary forces to incomes. This would help to explain the observed pattern of export, income, import deviations, together with the tendency for the *basic* British balance of payments to move into deficit in booms as compared with trend values, and into surplus in slumps so that Bank Rate was high in booms and low in slumps. Although the *current* account tended to improve in booms and worsen in slumps, it was less variable than the flow of lending abroad.[1] Furthermore, from 1879 to 1904 there was a distinct tendency for deviations in net home investment, in exports, and in overseas new issues, if the lead is allowed for, to concur; movements were confined to 1874–9 and 1904–9. All this coupled with the tendency for bunching in overseas issues deviations makes the assertion plausible that in the short run some considerable part of funds for overseas lending came from idle holdings, especially between 1879 and 1901.

In conclusion, the long-range effects of British overseas investment were dynamic. They served to increase the capacity of the borrowers to produce primary products, for which there were growing markets in Britain (and other parts of Europe) on account of rising population and real incomes, and at the expense of home production. The borrowers provided increased markets for British exports both in the construction period of projects and when their capacity to produce had expanded and rising primary product exports increased their ability to import manufactured goods. This two-way process of economic development was naturally not bilateral, although there were strong trading connections between many borrowing primary producers and Britain while multilateral effects also helped to expand British exports. As far as the 18–20 year alternating cycles of home and overseas investment were concerned, their principal importance lay in explaining how Britain could lend such large sums abroad without ties and not experience balance of payments strain to weaken adherence to the gold standard. It was tentatively suggested that there was a *trend* tendency for unemployment to rise when overseas investment expanded at the expense of home investment. However,

[1] *Ibid.*

it was in the short run that the variability of overseas lending was revealed as more productive of fluctuations in British activity. The British trade cycle was shown to be export-based and it was argued that one important influence on the variations in exports was the behaviour of deviations of *ex ante* overseas lending (measured by overseas issues) working through direct and more indirect methods. Any complete assessment of the precise role of overseas lending would require detailed review of the various fluctuations, which is beyond the scope of this paper. My aim is to draw attention to the likely role of *ex ante* overseas investment in British cycles by considering overall patterns, and to prompt further research. Nevertheless, a case has been established, I believe, for relating British cyclical fluctuations not only to variations in world market conditions and the domestic propensity to invest but to the varying pace of British overseas investment which in the particular economic environment of 1870–1914 reacted so strongly at times on the level of activity at home.

APPENDIX

Sources of series used:

Exports and Balance of Trade: B. R. Mitchell and Phyllis Deane, *Abstract of British Historical Statistics*, Cambridge, 1962.

Trade Union Unemployment: ibid.

Net Home Investment: C. H. Feinstein, 'Income and Investment in the United Kingdom 1856–1914', *Economic Journal*, LXXI (June 1961).

Net National Income: ibid.

Overseas Issues: C. Hobson, *The Export of Capital*, London, 1914.

Overseas Investment: A. H. Imlah, *Economic Elements in the Pax Britannica*, Harvard, 1958.

Value of World Trade Index: J. Tinbergen, *Business Cycles in the United Kingdom 1870–1914*, Amsterdam, 1951.

5 *Fluctuations in House-Building in Britain and the United States in the Nineteenth Century*[1]

H. J. HABAKKUK

[This article was first published in *The Journal of Economic History*, Vol. XXII, No. 2 (1962).]

The notion that an 'Atlantic Economy' developed in the nineteenth century does not depend simply on the large movements of capital and labour from Britain to the United States. For there were movements of comparable magnitude to other areas. If the economic relations of Britain and North America are to be regarded as distinctive, it is principally because of the reciprocal movement of investment and growth in the two areas.[2] The argument is that the periods of most rapid growth and intensive use of resources in the two economies were inversely related to each other, and that this alternation was established because there existed a common stock of resources, so that when one area drew rapidly on the stock it was at the expense of the other. At one time, investment in buildings and equipment in the United States was particularly rapid, and there was a heavy movement of migrants to America; in Britain the stream of migrants from the countryside was diverted from the industrial districts, and building and home investment were relatively depressed, but the vigorous demand for exports

[1] I have benefited from comments on an earlier draft of this paper by E. W. Cooney, J. R. T. Hughes, and S. B. Saul, and from discussion with D. Whitehead.

[2] This relationship has been identified and discussed by E. W. Cooney, 'Capital Exports and Investment in Building in Britain and the U.S.A.', *Economica*, New Series, XVI (November 1949), 347–54; by A. K. Cairncross. *Home and Foreign Investment, 1870–1913* (Cambridge University Press, 1953); and by B. Thomas, *Migration and Economic Growth* (Cambridge University Press, 1954), and a number of later studies.

facilitated the flow of funds abroad. In the next period, the position was reversed; development slackened in the United States, and there was a revival of domestic investment in Britain. This, as Phelps-Brown has said, 'is the pattern of the Atlantic Economy, dividing a common fund of incremental energies between its regions in varying proportions from time to time. Whether a house is built in Oldham depends on and is decided by whether a house goes up in Oklahoma.'[1]

So much importance has been attached to the reciprocal character of long swings in American and British domestic investment, and to the element of stability in the world economy which it afforded, that it may be worth while discussing the problem further. How early can the alternation of British and American investment be discerned? How far was it systematic as opposed to fortuitous? And, in so far as it was systematic, by what means was it established and maintained? The purpose of this essay is to consider these questions in relation to residential building, though some of the discussion will also apply to the types of public utility investment closely related to the growth of urban areas. Residential building is the form of investment where the case for alternation has been most clearly presented. It was also of comparable importance in the two economies, though it bulked larger and fluctuated more in America: in the United States, gross residential capital formation as a percentage of gross capital formation ranged from 30·1 per cent in 1891, a high year, to 18·6 per cent in 1903;[2] in England and Wales residential building averaged about 20 per cent of total new construction over the period 1886 to 1896.[3]

It is sometimes argued that both Britain and the United States had long cycles in residential building throughout the nineteenth century and that they were out of phase with each

[1] In a review of Thomas, *Migration and Economic Growth* in *Economic Journal*, LXIV, No. 256 (December 1954), 820.

[2] L. Grebler, D. M. Blank, and L. Winnick, *Capital Formation in Residential Real Estate* (National Bureau of Economic Research, Studies in Capital Formation and Financing, 1) (Princeton: Princeton University Press, 1956), p. 428.

[3] See Cairncross, *Home and Foreign Investment*, pp. 157, 169, 203.

other from the start.[1] So far as the United States is concerned, I do not wish to question the assumption that there were fluctuations in residential building of a twenty-year variety from early in the nineteenth century. The evidence so far available for the period before 1860 and even for the three following decades is thin, but there is a plausible reason for expecting such long swings, since the fluctuations in building were closely associated with the development booms which opened up the country, and these tended to occur every other trade cycle.[2]

Residential building in Britain took place mainly in areas already long settled, and there seems no obvious reason why its fluctuations over the country as a whole should have had a span of as long as twenty years, at least in the early decades of the century. Nor is there any compelling evidence that, up to the sixties at least, there were in fact long swings in total residential building over the country as a whole. The statistical evidence for the first half of the century is limited. The series for individual towns constructed by Weber do not effectively start until the 1850s, and even for this decade their coverage is narrow.[3] For the earlier decades there are only the figures of

[1] W. A. Lewis and P. J. O'Leary, 'Secular Swings in Production and Trade, 1870–1913', *Manchester School of Economic and Social Studies*, XXIII, No. 2 (May 1955), 113–52, believe that alternation can be discerned from the 1820s. Thomas dates the beginning of the inverse relation in 1847 (*Migration and Economic Growth*, p. 188).

[2] For the American figures see Thomas, *Migration and Economic Growth*, Appendix 4, Tables 108, 109. The data before 1860 are estimates made by Riggleman based on, at most, three cities. These are based for most years on permits for building (not house-building alone), but also take into account Riggleman's judgements based on information about mortgage activity, etc.

[3] For the British evidence see, besides Cairncross and Thomas, A. K. Cairncross and B. Weber, 'Fluctuations in Building in Great Britain, 1785–1849', *Economic History Review*, Second Series, IX, No. 2 (December 1956), 283–97; B. Weber, 'A New Index of Residential Construction and Long Cycles in House-Building in Great Britain, 1838–1950', *Scottish Journal of Political Economy*, II, No. 2 (June 1955); and J. H. Richards and J. Parry Lewis, 'House Building in the South Wales Coalfield, 1851–1913', *The Manchester School of Economic and Social Studies*, XXIV, No. 3 (September 1956), 289–300; Herbert W. Robinson, *The Economics of Building* (London: King, 1939), p. 100, gives the census figures of stocks of houses. The small increase in the stock of houses between 1841 and 1851 shown in the census figures is curious, since the railway building of this decade seems, as would be expected, to have stimulated internal migration.

the stock of houses at each census and certain series relating to building as a whole, for example, the volume of bricks derived from the excise figures and the imports of various kinds of timber. From these it seems reasonably clear that in Britain, house-building up to the 1860s rose over the period as a whole except for a check in the 1840s. The shape of the fluctuations in this growth can only be guessed, but the best guess that can be made is that they coincided generally with those of the trade cycle (cycles with a seven- to ten-year duration), not simply in the sense that house-building rose when trade revived and fell during trade depression, but also in the sense that there was no systematic tendency for house-building to be unusually vigorous or prolonged *every other* trade-cycle boom or unusually and protractedly depressed *every other* depression. From the nature of the evidence we cannot say this is confirmed by the brick index and the census figures on stocks of housing, but it is consistent with them, and there is some confirmatory evidence of a qualitative kind. There are signs of speculative domestic house building in the boom of 1824–5. A witness before the Select Committee of 1833 on Manufacturers, Commerce, and Shipping, commenting on severe depression in the building trade in 1826, suggested that all the houses required for 1826 were built in 1825; and other witnesses spoke of speculative building in Sheffield and Liverpool.[1] After a low level of building activity from 1827 to 1834,

---

(Cairncross, *Home and Foreign Investment*, pp. 70, 80.) It is possible that the census figures understate the number of houses built, since (*a*) before 1851 the interpretation of 'house' was left to the individual enumerator, and (*b*) there was some demolition of old houses as a result of railway building. Shannon's brick index shows an output in 1840–9 greater than in 1830–9 by nearly 25 per cent; but a large part of the output in the 1840s must have been absorbed by non-residential uses, particularly railway construction itself. If the small increase is genuine, the most likely explanation is that a very large amount of building had been done in the 1830s – the proportion of uninhabited houses per thousand in 1841 was higher than in 1811, 1821, and 1831 and than in 1851 and 1861. But the possibility cannot be ruled out that there were difficulties in obtaining finance in the two severe cyclical depressions of 1842 and 1847, and in the intervening railway boom which drew upon the type of savings most likely to be available for building.

[1] S. C. on Manufactures, Commerce and Shipping (1833), Qu. 1719, 4787, 2887, 2888. The year 1816 was also one of distress in building (Qu. 1777).

the rise in incomes between 1834 and 1836 caused an increase in residential building, particularly marked in the textile districts.[1] There seems to have been some revival of building in the uneven trade recovery from 1838 to 1840, but all the evidence suggests that the depression of 1842 brought a drastic fall. The course of residential building during the rest of the decade is not clear, but it is likely that a weak building boom coincided with the trade expansion; and the trade boom of the early 1850s was marked by a high level of building.[2]

In particular regions, fluctuations may well have had a different pattern. Matthews has suggested that in the period 1833–42 the long swings in British building activity were mainly regional, as opposed to the large national swings characteristic of the last quarter of the century.[3] Possibly there were long regional swings which bore no systematic relation to the trade cycle; in London the fall in building after the boom of 1825 was more severe and prolonged than for the country as a whole, and – presumably in part as a consequence – there was a rise in new houses from 1835–42 sustained throughout the trade-cycle depression.[4] But the building market in London was in several respects exceptional, and any long regional swings elsewhere are most likely to have occurred because so much building was done in one trade cycle that it was not absorbed until the next cycle but one; the swings took the form of a building boom every other trade revival. If these

---

[1] R. C. O. Matthews, *A Study in Trade-Cycle History: Economic Fluctuations in Great Britain, 1833–1842* (Cambridge: The University Press, 1954), pp. 116–17. The 1836 Act for the Regulation of Benefit Building Societies, passed because of the rapid increase in their number since the passing of the Friendly Society Act of 1834, suggests vigorous house-building.

[2] J. R. T. Hughes, *Fluctuations in Trade, Industry and Finance: A Study of British Economic Development, 1850–1860* (Oxford: Clarendon Press, 1960), pp. 225–7. It would be worth investigating the local press for evidence of building activity. See the Hampshire *Independent* for 6 September 1856. 'The progress made by Southampton during the past few years is strikingly apparent on all sides . . . whether we look at the new streets . . . or the erection of public buildings in every part of the town. We are astonished when passing through the new parts of the town to find the houses occupied before they are completed . . . proving incontestably the great demand for houses.'

[3] Matthews, *A Study in Trade-Cycle History*, p. 117.

[4] Cairncross and Weber, 'Fluctuations in Buildings', pp. 292–3.

regional swings were not synchronized – and in the still dis-united economy of the first half of the century there was no obvious mechanism to insure that all regions had their building booms in the same cycle – their effect would be to produce in the national aggregate fluctuations which coincided with the trade cycle.

Reasons can be suggested for a coincidence of building fluctuations with the trade cycle in the first half of the century. So far as the expansion phase of the cycle is concerned, it had unfavourable as well as favourable influences on building. On the one hand, the influx of migrants from the countryside into the industrial areas and the rise of industrial incomes increased the demand for houses. On the other hand, the increase in industrial activity competed for labour and building materials and drove up costs. Builders and potential house-purchasers had to face greater industrial competition for funds as indus-trialists, in order to finance expansion, drew in their loans and/or borrowed from local men who would otherwise have financed the construction or purchase of houses. Moreover, builders to some extent depended for finance on credits from those who supplied them with materials, and such credits were possibly less readily available in the later stages of a trade expansion; finance for building may have become more difficult before (or even without) a decline in the funds available for mortgages. Since finance is a larger part of total costs in the provision of houses than in the production of most other kinds of goods, building was particularly sensitive to such changes. The point is not merely that the decision to build houses, like the decision to undertake other forms of long-term investment, tended to be made only when recovery was well advanced, but that in its progress the recovery engendered forces unfavour-able to residential building as well as forces that were favour-able. In the first half of the century, however, favourable influences predominated over the country as a whole.[1] Migra-tion from the countryside took place mainly during the trade-

---

[1] Though the small increase in the stock of houses between 1841 and 1851 may be due to the fact that railway building competed with building for finance and labour more directly than did the dominant forms of investment in other cycles.

cycle booms. On the supply side, even at the height of a boom, unskilled building labour was abundant. The total supply of money and money substitutes during the boom was highly elastic, and since, down to about 1850, the return on consols tended to *fall* in periods of rising activity, we may reasonably deduce that there was a substantial increase in the funds available for mortgages.[1] Though finance may have limited building in particular areas, there is no evidence that house-building over the country as a whole was damped down by shortage of funds *before* the downturn of the trade cycle from the end of the Napoleonic wars to the 1850s. The net effect of a trade revival was to stimulate house-building.

During the trade-cycle depressions of the first part of the century, on the other hand, there were depressing influences on house-building from both the demand and supply side. The contraction of incomes was generally abrupt and severe. Moreover, because people were poorer than later in the century, they either doubled up in existing accommodation during depressions or went back to the villages, which was easier for a recently recruited labour force than for second- and third-generation urban workers. Migration to the towns died away.[2] Even where effective demand might have warranted a higher level of building in depression, it was difficult after the collapse of a trade-cycle boom to raise finance. The downturn in the early decades of the century was normally accompanied by a commercial and financial panic, as a result of which there was a rapid contraction of funds for all types of investment – house-building and industrial investment as well. Because the English banking system in the earlier nineteenth century was unstable and the range of assets available was narrow, the desire for liquidity was very strong, and it absorbed even the funds

[1] Possibly, also, to a greater extent than later in the century, house-building was financed by industrialists out of profits.

[2] Hansard (3rd Series), LXLV, 118, 1248. Tooke attributed the depressed state of agricultural workers in 1844 'to the accumulating results of the interruption of the customary migration from the agricultural to the manufacturing districts, during the long and severe depression of the latter'. (Thomas Tooke and William Newmarch, *A History of Prices*, 6 vols. in 4 (reproduced from the original and published New York: Adelphi, 1928), IV, 56–57.)

available for new mortgages and led to reluctance to renew them. (It also led to the sale of consols which is why, from the 1780s to the 1850s, the yield on consols fell during booms and rose during depressions.) The trade-cycle crisis broke the speculative building boom and made many builders bankrupt; when the immediate effects of the crisis had worn off and finance again became available for building, the industry was in the doldrums. How far building booms ceased because of the fall in demand during depression and how far they were cut short by financial crises in circumstances in which demand would have warranted a continuation it is impossible to say. The only point I wish to make here is that the nature of the trade-cycle downturn in this period tailored fluctuations in building to fit the trade cycle.

So long as this was the case, there was no regular alternation between British and American building fluctuations.[1] British building tended to move with the trade cycle, and American building with the development booms. These development booms tended to occur roughly every other trade cycle, and since there was a rough synchronization of the trade cycle in the two countries the peaks in building tended to coincide as often as not. There are some signs of alternation in the 1860s – the British had a marked building boom in the early 1860s, while, because of the Civil War, the American building boom was deferred to the second half of the decade. But the signs are not very marked. Building fluctuations in the two countries did not become clearly out of phase until the 1870s. In both America and Britain, building rose in the trade revival of the late 1860s and was high during 1869–72; but American building declined abruptly after 1872, while building in Britain, though it fell slightly in 1873, rose again to new heights between 1874 and 1876. This is the first unambiguous instance of a building

---

[1] There seems to be no evidence for the view of Lewis and O'Leary ('Secular Swings in Production', p. 176) that alternation was evident from the 1820s. Thomas's view that the alternation started as early as 1847, and that English building was low in the 1850s when American building was high, is based on the assumption that railway miles added in England are an index of building. His conclusions, so far as residential building in the 1850s is concerned, are difficult to reconcile with the census figures for housing in 1851 and 1861.

boom in Britain coinciding with a trough in American building. Thereafter the building cycles continued to alternate in the way Cairncross and Thomas have described, with British building low in the eighties, rising in the 1890s to a peak in 1903 and low again between 1907 and the outbreak of war, and American building moving in the reverse direction.[1]

Even of these periods of alternation it should be observed that the available indices, which are primarily of building in urban areas, probably exaggerate the extent to which building fluctuations in the two countries diverged. In Britain, except in certain of the coal fields, most of the urban growth in the second half of the nineteenth century took place in or around centres which were already urban in 1851. In the United States, on the other hand, more of the urban growth took the form of the appearance of new large towns; an index based on the figures for the administrative areas of towns is in general likely to be a more accurate measure of American than of British building. Furthermore, when there was a significant change in the proportions of suburban building in the two countries, the existing indices would mislead. In the 1900s a large amount of building in England was suburban. Weber's index of thirty-four major English towns therefore understates total English house-building in this decade, as indeed is evident from the figures of intercensus increase. Between 1901 and 1911 the number of houses in England and Wales as a whole rose by 12·5 per cent and in 'urban districts', that is, the smaller urban areas, by as much as 19·2 per cent. These figures, while they do not necessarily indicate a cyclical pattern different from that in Weber's figures, do suggest a higher level of building.

Thus alternation is confined to the forty or so years before 1914. It will be observed, also, that the beginning of this alternating came about because of a change in the character of British building fluctuations, by which they ceased to follow the path of the trade cycle and became longer and more widely

[1] There was also some alternation in the 1920s and 1930s, with English building relatively low in the first decade and high in the second; but this period falls outside the scope of this essay.

spaced in time. The building boom which started in the later
1860s is the first clear case in which the national peak in English
house-building occurred a considerable time after the peak of
the trade cycle. That this building boom was unprecedented is
suggested by the fact that the proportion of uninhabited to
inhabited houses in 1881 was much the highest in the century –
eighty per thousand.

At first sight it seems obvious enough that British building
fluctuations were accommodating themselves to the American.
But the British cycle in the later nineteenth century was the
product of its own previous history as well as of contemporary
events in the United States, and there are reasons why it should
have changed its character quite apart from any events in the
United States. More specifically, there are reasons of domestic
origin why the relation between British building fluctuations
and the trade cycle should have changed and, in particular, why
a long wave of building activity should have appeared.

There were first of all changes which, in the later nineteenth
century, weakened the influences which stimulated building
during a trade expansion. The association between internal
migration and trade expansion became less close. Not only
was urbanization more rapid in the first half of the century, but
it was in this period that the contribution of migration to
urbanization was relatively greatest; and in this sense building
was more subject to the influence of migration. There were
changes in the social composition of the migrants in the later
decades of the century: to judge from the rapid growth of
middle-class towns in the twenty years before 1900, there was an
increase in the proportion of middle-class migrants, and their
movement was less directly dependent on trade fluctuations.[1]

While the favourable influences exerted during the boom on
the demand side were becoming less powerful, the unfavourable influences exerted on the availability of finance and on
costs became more powerful. There are signs that finance had

[1] Discussion on R. Price Williams, 'On the Increase of Population in England
and Wales', *Journal of the Royal Statistical Society*, XLIII, Part III (September
1880), 500–1; T. A. Welton, *England's Recent Progress* (London: Chapman &
Hall, 1911), pp. 564–9.

become a restraint on residential building in the 1850s and 1860s. In the boom of the 1860s, house-building was curtailed before the crisis of the trade cycle, and it was suggested that this was the result of difficulty in negotiating mortgages. 'Persons can now realize from 5 to 6 per cent very readily upon loans, or merely by deposits at joint-stock banks, and, therefore, are not to be satisfied with 4 or 5 from builders encumbered with the business of mortgages and other securities.'[1] In 1865 and 1866 building was again cut off by shortage of funds well before the boom broke. Finance became more difficult during the boom as a result of the development of a more stable and unified banking system – particularly the growth of joint-stock banks with more considered policies about reserves – and the increasing assumption by the Bank of England of central banking functions. Possibly, too, the increasing perfection of the capital market worked to the disadvantage of house-building in the boom. There were more places in the first half of the century than in the second where builders and house-purchasers found it easy to obtain funds during a boom simply because local money men could find little else to do with their money. It also became more difficult for builders to obtain labour during the boom; there were complaints of general labour shortage in the 1850s, and the contemporary already quoted attributed the decline in building in January 1857 to higher wages as well as higher interest rates. Probably there was some general tendency for housing to be squeezed at the height of the boom, as the reserve army of labour was depleted and as supplies of credit became less responsive in the upswing of the cycle. Resources were less easily able to accommodate an increase in all types of investment during a boom, and pressure was greater in the 1850s and 1860s than in the twenties and thirties.

Changes in the methods of financing house-building made it more vulnerable to high interest rates and shortage of funds at the height of the boom. A witness before a Commons Committee said in 1857:

[1] A letter in *The Builder* of January 1857, quoted by Tooke and Newmarch, *History of Prices*, VI, 175–6.

Forty years ago what houses were built upon speculation were built out of the savings and the profits of builders upon their ordinary jobbing business, and it answered very well at that day. But at present the general practice is to build upon a large scale . . . and raising money upon mortgage as the buildings proceed. Almost the whole of Belgravia and Tyburnia, and the countless thousands of villas round London, are built upon that principle. A man makes an arrangement with some solicitor, who has clients ready to advance money, and he says, 'As you go on we will advance a certain portion on Mortgage.' That is the way that the builder generally finances.[1]

If this witness was right, speculative housing at the end of the Napoleonic wars was financed by the savings and profits of the jobbing business more than by mortgage. This dependence on the builders' savings and profits was probably a temporary phenomenon – it does not seem to have been characteristic of building in the eighteenth century – due not only to the strong demand in the jobbing business in the years after 1815 but to the exceptional difficulty of raising money upon mortgage in the later stages of the Napoleonic wars and the time needed afterwards to re-establish fully the links between the building industry and the mortgage market. But, whatever the cause, it seems likely that by the 1850s a larger proportion of building was done by builders building ahead of demand for a market financed by mortgages, as opposed to men building with their own capital. Since the mortgage rate was, from the nature of the instrument, more stable than the industrial or commercial profit rate and the rate on, for example, commercial bills, the relative attraction, to the investor, of loans to builders tended to diminish in the trade-cycle boom and to increase during the slump. Housing suffered in the competition for funds not merely because the stickiness of rents made it difficult to pass on any increase in costs, but also because mortgage rates were sticky – solicitors had only heard of one rate. Moreover, the development of joint-stock banking, while it may have made

[1] S. C. of 1857, Qu. 5414.

it easier for builders to obtain advances, also made the bank deposit an alternative asset to the mortgage. These changes made the building industry more sensitive to given fluctuations in the supply of finance, and, if this had been the only determinant, building fluctuations would have been anti-cyclical.

These developments meant that in the 1850s and 1860s not all the houses were built during the boom that were warranted by the level of demand during the boom or even by the lower level of demand after the downturn of the cycle. Independent of events abroad, there was some frustrated demand which tended to sustain this form of investment into the trade-cycle depression. Though the high building of the mid-seventies is the first clear instance of a boom in building of longer duration that the trade cycle, the revival of building after 1866 was sufficiently prompt to suggest that it was stimulated by a backlog of demand from the previous period of industrial activity.

For building to be sustained after the downturn of the trade-cycle boom, effective demand for houses had to be sustained and funds had to be available. The growing stability of the banking system after mid-century and the increase in the range of assets available, while they reduced the power of building to compete for funds during a boom, greatly improved its position during a depression. The downturn ceased to be accompanied by a general commercial and financial convulsion. The year 1866 was the last of the genuine panics. Moreover, since persons and institutions held a greater diversity of assets, the pressure for liquidity in the later nineteenth century was no longer exerted on bonds and mortgages, but on short-term securities. Indeed, in depression there was a shift to funds *into* such assets as consols and mortgages, and this is why the yield on consols in the second half of the century, in contrast to the first, moved in sympathy with industrial activity and fell during depressions.[1]

---

[1] This is the main explanation of the change in the behaviour of consols over the trade cycle noted by Sir William Beveridge, 'The Trade Cycle in Britain Before 1850', *Oxford Economic Papers*, No. 3 (February 1940), 91.

Thus the increase in the stability of English financial institutions tended to detach building from the trade cycle. In the earlier decades of the century, because of imperfections in the capital market, housebuilding during a trade-cycle boom had a full head in some areas and was constrained in others; but once the boom had broken, conditions became unfavourable to building in all areas, partly because of a general unwillingness to lend and partly because the contraction of incomes reduced demand for housing. The increased availability of finance for building in depression in the second half of the century allowed building to go ahead in those areas where, even in depression, demand conditions were favourable.

Absence of a commercial panic affected not only the availability of finance for building, but also effective demand for houses. The point is not merely that stringencies of the boom meant there was an unsatisfied demand for houses at the level of income prevailing during the cyclical boom, but that the level of income was better sustained during the depression. The possibility should also be considered that the change in the character of British building fluctuations, whereby they ceased to coincide with the trade cycle, was partly due to an increase in the relative importance of the type of area in which, even in the earlier nineteenth century, the net effect of trade revival was to inhibit rather than stimulate residential building.

These changes in the character of the trade cycle in Britain would lead one to expect a change in the response of building to the trade cycle. But why, it may be asked, should they produce *long swings* in building? Building fluctuations may be related to the trade cycle in a number of different ways and still remain of the same length as the trade cycle. They may be positively and synchronously tied to the cycle; but they may also be inversely related; or industrial demand for resources may regularly depress building in the second half of trade-cycle expansions and slack industrial demand stimulate it in the second half of recessions. Or, again, the favourable and unfavourable effects on building of the various phases of the cycle may offset each other, and the balance of trade-cycle influences might shift over time between these possibilities without affecting the length of building fluctuations.

The changes I have examined in fact produced long waves because the shift in the balance of favourable and unfavourable forces was gradual, so that, at some point of time, the building boom came to overlap the trade cycle, rising during trade expansion but continuing to rise after the cyclical downturn. Once this had happened there was an increase in the number of regional long cycles, since, after such a long wave, building would skip the immediately following trade revival. Once the pattern of building fluctuations had been modified in this way there was no reason why it should revert to its previous shape.

To the extent that these regional waves were not synchronized, they would tend to produce greater steadiness in the national aggregate, the building boom in some regions overlapping one trade cycle, and those in other regions overlapping the trade cycle immediately following. But so long as the two classes of region were not equally important as centres of building, there would be a tendency for long swings to appear in the national aggregate. As the British economy became more closely integrated geographically in the course of the nineteenth century, it is probable that there was an increasing degree of synchronization between regional building fluctuations. But quite apart from this, an increase in the number of regional long swings would tend to lengthen, as well as moderate, the swings for the country as a whole.

I wish to suggest that the appearance of the first long wave in the 1870s is primarily to be explained by influences of this kind. The depressing influences on building during the trade revival of 1869–72, while sufficient to leave a backlog of demand for housing, did not prevent an increase in building, and the favourable influences after the cyclical downturn of 1873 boosted building to a peak in 1876. So much building had been done between 1869 and 1876 that in most areas there was little scope for a revival of building in the trade revival of 1879–82; there had been built not only the houses needed at the level of incomes prevailing in the 1870s but a large part of those that were needed at the income level of the early eighties.

There is another general development which one might expect to have produced a longer rhythm in British building fluctuations – the increasing importance of suburban building, particularly for middle-class people. At first, builders filled in the settled areas of a town and then made piecemeal additions on the outskirts; in this way, a town might grow very large without the provision of new transport facilities, for increasing dispersion of industry within an urban area could allow inhabitants to live near enough their work to walk to it. There came a point beyond which further expansion of the town involved the provision of trams or trains, and additional public utilities. Whether at this point transport and housing moved simultaneously into the suburbs under a common stimulus or whether one or the other was the initiating influence depended not only on the accidents of local history but on the form of transport. The increased use of horse-trams at the end of the seventies and the early eighties seems to have been a *consequence* of the housing boom of the mid-seventies; these lines enabled people to live farther out – people could now walk to the terminus – but the lines were very short and did not generally reach the suburbs and did not stimulate much building on the outskirts in the eighties. On the other hand, the boom in electric trams at the end of the 1890s, though we cannot say how far it influenced the volume as opposed to the location of building, was primarily an independent stimulus and not a response to new house-building. In the case of suburban railway lines, there are instances where lines were built ahead of the house-building which was to justify them. But whether transport and other facilities or the houses came first, building was likely to have a longer rhythm than that of an earlier period whenever urban expansion involved investment in developing a new area. Once the minimum of transport facilities and public utilities had been provided, the area provided opportunities for a large amount of building; builders could expect not only profits on the sale of houses, but also gains from rising land values; and they could expect such gains more confidently than builders in existing urban areas where the price of land was more likely to discount the future. Builders thus had an inducement to buy land during trade depression, when it was cheap, and hold it ready to develop at the first sight of an increase in demand for houses. The prospects of capital gain might insure that such development, once started, proceeded even after house prices had ceased to rise. Where new houses were being built in the suburbs and people were migrating from the central areas of towns, the number of empty houses in the centre might increase for several years without affecting the profitability of suburban building in the way in which a comparable amount of building nearer the central area would have done. (In these circumstances a high proportion of empty houses might not be a sign of over-building but merely of the location of new building.) After such building activity, a renewed influx of migrants from the country into the towns would find a concentration of empty houses in the central urban area which would need to be taken up before there was a demand for new housing, and this again would tend to lengthen the intervals between building booms.

It might be objected at this stage that to confine attention to residential building is to beg the question. For long swings have been found in other items of British domestic investment in the later nineteenth century – in the expenditure of local authorities, in railways, and – though on more fragile evidence – in industrial investment. Are the long swings in these items also to be explained by reference to domestic influences? Is it not more probable that they were the result of systematic interaction with American long swings? And, in this case, is it not likely that it was the long swings in these other items of domestic investment which caused the long swings in residential building?

It is indeed likely that, in a developed country like Britain, fluctuations in residential building would be a passive response to movements in other items of investment to a greater degree than in a country still in process of settlement. But the movements to which they responded were, I wish to suggest, those of the trade cycle; and the appearance of long swings outside

E

residential building is itself the result of changes in the character of the cycle.

Because British trade cycles ceased to come to an end with a commercial convulsion or financial panic, the forces sustaining investment and income after the downturn were much more effective than they were earlier in the century. Lumpy projects begun in the boom needed to be completed and provided with ancillary equipment; projects completed in the boom were filled in. Some fresh investment was undertaken as the result of opportunities created by boom investment, for example, the external economies resulting from railway building and the extension of knowledge and know-how resulting from a mining boom or the introduction of new types of blast furnace. Projects deferred because of high costs were taken up when costs fell, and perhaps financed from the high profits of the preceding boom. For example, English railway investment was high in the mid-seventies partly because of the abnormally high profits of the preceding boom, and because track, once started, had to be finished and furnished with new rolling stock.

Influences of this kind are, of course, present in any cyclical depression, but in England they operated more immediately in the late than in the early nineteenth century. And in the late nineteenth century they operated more strongly in Britain than in America or in other overseas regions whose banking systems were more vulnerable and whose booms had a stronger 'mania' element. There has recently been some suggestion that in England after the 1860s the trade cycle was not an independent phenomena but simply the result of lack of synchronization between the long swings in foreign and domestic investment.[1] The view taken here is the reverse of this: it was the long swings which were the epiphenomena and the trade cycles the reality, in the sense that when the character of the individual cycles has been explained there is no residue which needs to be attributed to the behaviour of a long cycle. The appearance of alternation in British and American long swings is the result of the fact that British trade cycles no longer came to a violent end but the American ones often did.

[1] Matthews, *A Study in Trade-Cycle History.*

This section has been an attempt to attribute the appearance of long waves in British building in the later nineteenth century to domestic influences; though there are obvious dangers in attempting to isolate the domestic elements in an economy so dependent upon foreign trade, some such changes as we have described might be reasonably expected even in a closed economy. Nor can the possibility be ruled out that the inverse relationship which these long waves proved to bear to the long waves in American building was fortuitous, for the inverse relationship is not all that exact; it is only a few fluctuations that are in question, and the logical possible number of relationships between them is small.[1]

Systematic alternation existed in so far as the two areas drew on a common stock of resources. Where building is concerned the resources of most interest are migrants and funds, though if we were considering investment as a whole, certain types of skill and capital equipment would have to be considered.

The suggestion most commonly made is that the alternation was established and maintained by fluctuations in the number of migrants. The simplest case would be one in which the building cycle in both countries was determined by migration, that is, where migrants depressed the demand for British houses when they left Britain and raised the demand for American houses when they entered the United States.

So far as the United States was concerned it seems clear that fluctuations in residential building were sensitive to fluctuations in the volume of immigration from all sources. An increase in immigration did not *initiate* a revival of building; the revival was started by changes in migration within the United States which preceded changes in immigration, that is, the economic events which attracted immigrants would in any case have caused some boom in building. But the immigrants strengthened and prolonged the boom. Since the periods of heavy emigration from Britain tended to coincide with the periods of heavy immigration from all sources into the United States, we should expect the periods when American

[1] Any alternation in the 1860s was due to the American Civil War, which was fortuitous in this context.

building was active to have coincided with heavy emigration from Britain. This by itself, however, would not have been sufficient to produce an alternation of building cycles.

For the connection between emigration and building fluctuations in Britain is much less obvious. It is clear that fluctuations in the number of emigrants were too small to have had a direct influence on fluctuations of activity in the British building industry; for the rate of increase in *total population* (or, what is more relevant, the total number of households) was very little lower in the periods of heavy emigration, and the absolute increase was as large as in periods of low emigration.

The argument in the case of Britain, however, does not rest on fluctuations in total emigration, but on the relation of these to the rate of urbanization in Britain. The argument has rested on changes not in total population but in urban population, and the supposition has been that British towns grew most rapidly in the periods of low emigration. As Cairncross puts it 'urban expansion and colonisation tended to alternate with each other in successive decades'; or as Thomas says, 'when a relatively large number of people are leaving the country, internal mobility is low'.[1]

There are really three distinct issues involved:

(*a*) How far, in fact, did internal migration alternate with emigration?

(*b*) In so far as it did, how far were the alternations causally connected? How far, for example, were the variations in the volume of internal migration in Britain determined by fluctuations in external migration as compared to changes in the disparity between English agricultural and urban incomes, changes in the costs of internal migration and in the geographical distribution of industry?

(*c*) How great an influence did changes in internal migration in Britain have upon the British building cycle?

In dealing with the first point we are handicapped by paucity of data, for though there are annual figures relating to emigra-

[1] Cairncross, *Home and Foreign Investment*, pp. 68, 74; Thomas, *Migration and Economic Growth*, p. 173.

tion, for internal migration there are only the decennial census figures which sum up the net result of the preceding decade. The movements inside each decade can only be guessed. There were clearly years in the nineteenth century when internal migration and emigration moved together; the boom of 1869–73 saw both urbanization and expansion of the area of overseas settlement. But there were also occasions where there was alternation. The position in the 1870s is ambiguous; it is not clear whether the rise in English residential building activity in 1874–7 indicates an increase in migration to the towns in these years, or accommodation for people who had migrated in the previous trade-cycle boom. There must have been some increase in migration to the towns in the later 1880s but it was slight compared with the increase in emigration; 1894 to 1901 was a period of relatively low emigration, and probably of considerable internal migration. The years after 1900 saw considerable emigration and relatively small net urbanization. From 1880 on, therefore, there is a plausible case for supposing that English urbanization alternated with American 'colonization'.

At first sight the notion that, when migration to the towns was low and emigration high, the high emigration *caused* the low migration, seems obvious common sense; if people had not gone abroad a sufficient number would have gone to the towns to make a significant difference to the level of residential building in England. But the assumptions underlying this view need checking. The main assumption is that English towns competed with the United States in a common reservoir of potential migrants from the English countryside, the size of which was determined by fairly long-term factors. When one competitor made more rapid claims on this reservoir, the flow to the other fell off; the level of income and opportunity prevailing at any time in English towns and in the United States made more difference to the division of the stream of migrants between them than to the size of the stream.[1]

But it is possible to conceive other situations. The total

---

[1] B. Thomas, 'Wales and the Atlantic Economy', *Scottish Journal of Political Economy*, VI, No. 3 (November 1959), 169–71.

stream of migrants may have been very sensitive to short-term changes in economic opportunity, so that, when both British towns and America grew simultaneously, one did not obtain migrants at the expense of the other but both obtained them at the expense of a more rapid flight from the English country-side. A high level of migration to one area might indeed, by force of example and by loosening social bonds, induce some people to migrate to the other. Of course when one competitor was prosperous and the other depressed, the prosperous one would get the migrants, but one could not say that the one area was depriving the other of migrants, for if both had been depressed neither of them would have had many; and if both had been active both would have had all the migrants they wanted. As a third possibility one can suppose that English towns and the United States each drew on its own particular pool of migrants, in which case, even if neither pool were elastic, the demands of one area would not compete with those of the other.

These are theoretical possibilities, but they correspond to three recognizable types of motive and situation. There was the man who was determined to leave the English countryside in any case sooner or later, whose decision when to leave was determined by random factors like the harvest or his age, but whose choice of destination was very sensitive to the relative attractiveness of the English towns and the United States at the moment when he decided to leave. At the other extreme was the man who decided on one particular destination, the timing of whose move depended on the varying conditions in that destination. There must, for example, have been many men for whom the choice was to emigrate or to stay in the country-side – men who waited for good conditions before emigrating but who would not be attracted to the English towns by any conjunction of circumstances. There may also have been people, especially among the older people, whose preference was very strongly for the English town and who never seriously considered emigrating. In between these groups are people with a range of different preferences about the timing of their migration and their destination, whose decisions on both points were subject to short-term variations in economic conditions.

It cannot therefore be assumed without further argument that if emigration had been lower in any period internal migration would have been very much higher. It may be, for example, that in the mid-seventies migrants moved to English towns because activity in them remained high, not because emigration had become less attractive. It is even more likely that the more rapid urbanization of the later nineties would have taken place even in the face of larger emigration; the towns grew because they were seats of innovation not because migrants were diverted from America; and if the demand of the primary producing areas for migrants had been higher they would probably have got them from other countries or by a higher level of migration from the English countryside rather than at the expense of English urbanization. Even for the period after 1900, when it seems most obvious from the census figures that emigration was at the expense of the growth of towns, there are some qualifications to be made. In the first place, the loss to the urban areas as defined for census purposes represents in part simply the growth of suburbs and not a loss to towns in the wider economic sense. In the second place, the centres of industrial expansion in these years – the coal fields of South Wales and Yorkshire, the Lancashire cotton towns, and centres of new industry like Coventry – attracted a considerable number of migrants: they were evidently able to compete with the attractions of emigration. Nevertheless it is reasonable to suppose that, but for attractions abroad, those urban areas where demand for labour was not expanding, and areas like London from which labour was migrating, would have had a higher level of building. Probably also in the 1880s, people would have left agriculture in any case, but in the absence of good opportunities abroad they would have gone to English towns.

There is, therefore, some sense in saying that in the 1880s and in the 1900s a large number of people emigrated who would otherwise have gone to (or stayed in) the English towns. This was probably a new feature. In the first half of the century emigration was much more a *pis aller;* migrants went to English towns in booms and emigration tended to be highest in depression; of the early period it would be truer to say that when migration and emigration alternated, emigration was determined by internal migration.

But even where the fluctuations in internal migration after, say, the 1870s were dominated by those in emigration, it by no means follows, even in this period, that the English building cycle was dominated by internal migration. There are two objections which must be met before this view can be accepted. In the first place, though there was a fall of about 10 per cent in the absolute numbers of the population of the rural areas as a whole from 1861 to 1901, it was only in the 1880s that the fall was significant, and between 1901 and 1911 there was an increase.[1] In these circumstances, why should *migration* – as opposed to the increase of total population, which has already been ruled out as an inadequate explanation – have had any effect on the total demand for housing? Would not the migrants to the towns have had to find accommodation even if they had stayed in the countryside? In the second place, many of the migrants were young and unskilled, who must have found difficulty in obtaining work and have earned low wages at first; many were single and would naturally fit into existing households, often enough with urban relations. This is to say the newcomers may have represented only a very small effective demand for new houses.

To the first objection there are reasonable answers. Though in the *aggregate* the absolute fall in rural population may not have been significant for our purposes, there were several areas where there *was* such a significant fall. On the most rigorous assumptions, therefore, some of the movements to the towns represented a net addition to the need for houses; if the migrants had stayed in the country, the existing house-room there would have been ample for them. Even when there was no absolute fall in the rural population, the additional population was more likely to stimulate a demand for new houses if it

[1] A. L. Bowley, 'Rural Population in England and Wales', *Journal of the Royal Statistical Society*, LXXVII, Pt. VI (May 1914), 605–6.

moved to the towns than if it stayed in the countryside. For country accommodation was probably more stretchable. It is true that conditions in Liverpool or Manchester suggest that accommodation was very stretchable in some towns. But migrants came from each of a very large number of villages and went to a small number of towns, that is, the sources of migrants were diffused but their destinations were concentrated. So it was easier to accommodate a man in his village than when he moved to the town. The migrant to the town, furthermore, was more likely to have to *pay* for additional accommodation among strangers; had he stayed in his village he would probably have been fitted in, at little or no cost to him, with his family or with relatives. Then again movement to the town must have meant for the migrants as a whole an increase in money incomes, and therefore an increase in money demand for houses. Moreover, it is not only the effective demand of the newcomers to the urban areas which must be considered: the demand of the people pushed out of the older parts of the towns by these newcomers was probably substantial. Immigrants from the country concentrated in the areas where housing was poorest, areas on the verge of becoming slums, and their influx led to the exodus of some of the existing occupants and to the extension of suburbs; migration of the countryside caused a building boom in Didsbury rather than in central Manchester, just as migration from the Mississippi causes a housing boom in Westchester not in Harlem. For all these reasons a shift of people from country to town probably meant an increase in the demand for houses and not merely a change in the place where houses were demanded. Finally, there is no doubt that a given increase in demand for house-room was more likely to be met by additional building when it was exerted in the town than when it was exerted in the village, because the building industry was organized to meet urban rather than rural demand. For one thing, urban demand was more concentrated. For another, in the countryside, a substantial part of the housing was provided by the landowners at low rent and in part payment of wages, and the supply of houses was not determined by market considerations, so that even a rural wage earner who could have afforded a better house would, in many villages, not have found one available.[1]

There is also an answer to the second objection. The argument is not that an influx of migrants into English towns in the seventies by itself stimulated a housing boom, or even that the slower pace of urban immigration in the 1880s by itself prevented one. The argument is that in the mid-seventies, when finance was easy and construction costs low, and when there was a backlog to be made up, building was able to continue at a high level because demand was reinforced by a stream of immigrants; migration into the towns explains not why the building boom started but why it continued so long. Contrariwise, in the mid-eighties, when there were signs of a revival of building, the argument is that it did not proceed farther because demand was no longer braced by newcomers. There is, therefore, no reason in principle why migration should not have made the English building cycle alternate with the American, but the discussion suggests that the variations would need to have been very substantial to have had this effect.

Overseas regions competed with the British building industry for funds as well as for migrants. I argued, in an earlier section, that house-building had to compete for finance with certain other types of domestic investment. The point which may be urged about foreign investment in the later nineteenth century is that it was a more serious and direct competitor for the funds available for English house-building. There had developed during the eighteenth century, principally because of the growth of the national debt, a substantial class of passive investors. The numbers and resources of this class were enormously extended during the wars against France between 1792 and 1815, and interest payments on the debt further increased their accumulations. Tooke, writing of the early 1850s, refers to 'the increased wealth of the country, and the peculiar social

---

[1] 'The general complaint all over the country with regard to rural matters and the agricultural industry is the want of accommodation; old dwellings are condemned on account of their condition, and it does not pay to build new ones.' (Cd. 2751 of 1905, Qu. 21698.)

arrangements which confine a considerable part of the accumulations to investment in the public funds.'[1] These savings were not readily diverted into the London money market; for most of the century English industry did not make large claims upon them, partly because its own savings were sufficient for the increase in capacity which it wished to undertake, partly because it could not easily offer securities which were attractive to the passive investor. The coming of limited liability did not fundamentally alter this position. The passive investor favoured government securities or investments of a public utility type – transport improvements, urban developments, housing – investments financed largely by bonds or mortgages. Foreign investment was financed in ways which were attractive to this type of investor. A large part of it consisted of government borrowing; much of the private borrowing was of a public utility type, and the need to obtain funds often compelled foreigners to finance projects which were not of this type by the issue of bonds bearing a fixed interest.

There was, therefore, a substantial amount of saving done by passive investors who switched, not between British industry and British public utilities, but between British public utilities and foreign investment. Substantial shifts in the disposition of new funds could take place with small or even negligible changes in return; a mere increase in the relevant type of securities might be sufficient.

Until the 1850s and 1860s the claims of foreign investment on these *rentier* savings were circumscribed, partly because few foreign countries were developing so rapidly that they needed to borrow heavily, and partly because a high degree of risk still attached to their securities. There was, moreover, a strong domestic demand for such savings. Up to 1815 the increase in government debt absorbed much of them. In several of the trade revivals, the dominant form of investment was of a public utility type – canals and turnpikes in the 1790s and railways in the 1830s and 1840s; even in the revival of the fifties railways raised large amounts of capital, and there was in addition government borrowing during the Crimean War. It is·

[1] Tooke and Newmarch, *History of Prices*, V, 315.

true that even before the 1850s there was competition between British and foreign investment; foreign investment tended to fluctuate with the trade cycle and influenced the size of the pool of *rentier* savings available for domestic investment; it is significant that the first large foreign investment boom of the nineteenth century occurred during the trade revival of the mid-1820s, when the pace at home was made by metals and textiles and not by public utilities. But by and large the main competition which English housing had to meet in the first half of the century came from other domestic claimants rather than from abroad.

In the decades after the 1850s, foreign demand for the savings of English *rentiers* grew and the risks probably diminished. So far as domestic investment was concerned, the main demand for such savings now came from housing and closely allied urban developments, and some of the money which in the 1840s would have gone into English railways, in the 1870s went into mortgages. But domestic mortgages, though more attractive than other available domestic alternatives, were in several respects unsatisfactory: they were unhomogeneous and the market in them was very imperfect; it was difficult to adjust the terms on which they were contracted in such a way as adequately to discount this disadvantage whenever supplies of foreign bonds, especially government bonds, became available. In the competition for the saving of the passive investor, domestic housing was much less powerful *vis-à-vis* foreign investment than domestic railways had been in the 1830s and 1840s. This indeed is one of the reasons for the magnitude of British foreign investment between 1870 and 1914 – with one exception the booms in England were dominated by developments in industry, in which the English passive investor did not participate. Except when the government was borrowing during the Boer War, there were few domestic claimants for *rentier* savings sufficiently attractive to stand up to the competition of foreign borrowers, since the market in foreign securities was well organized.

Since most of the English trade-cycle booms coincided with high activity in the primary producing areas, foreign competition with housing mortgages was exerted in the boom. While English trade expansions no longer ended with a financial crisis, those in primary producing areas usually did, so that during a depression, *rentier* savings were very sharply deflected back to such secure domestic assets as mortgages. Thus the character and timing of foreign investment reinforced both the pressure on building finance during the trade-cycle boom and the availability of funds for building during the following depression.

Exactly how sensitive the flow of funds was must await investigation. It depended partly on the particular foreign security: on the face of it one would expect English mortgages and the securities of Argentinian railways to have appealed to different classes of investors. It must also have depended on the scale of operations of the builders and of the solicitors, who negotiated many of the mortgages, which varied from area to area. In some areas, for example in South Wales, most house-owners owned only a few houses, bought from the profits of a small business – a public house, etc. – or with a mortgage financed from such sources. One would not expect such people readily to divert their savings into foreign bonds during a boom. On the other hand, in the 1880s, as J. D. Bailey has shown, Scottish funds were switched directly out on Scottish into Australian mortgages.[1] This evidence relates particularly to a switch between Australia and Scotland, and may be exceptional since Australians borrowed much more on mort-gage than other primary producing areas, and Scottish in-vestors were more dependent on solicitors than the English. But English investors also invested heavily in the debentures of Anglo-Australian land mortgage companies and placed large sums on deposit with Australian financial institutions. At the end of the 1880s there was no difficulty in inducing English-men to lend on Australian debentures at $3\frac{1}{2}$ or 4 per cent. It is a fair presumption that there were many passive investors who readily switched their savings between home and foreign assets of comparable types.

[1] J. D. Bailey, 'Australian Borrowing in Scotland in the Nineteenth Century', *Economic History Review*, Second Series, XII, No. 2 (December 1959), 268–79.

There is some general probability about the notion that foreign demand for funds was at the expense of building finance. Very large sums were invested abroad in periods of heavy foreign investment. Some of these funds must have come from saving out of increased incomes, but it seems likely from the national income figures that a large part must have come from a switch from some item of domestic investment. The increase in foreign investment and the fall in building and public utility-type investment are of the same general order of magnitude, and this in itself suggests that the switch was at the expense of building. Finally, the existence of a large pool of savings, the size of which was not sensitive to changes in income, which could be drawn into the finance of building, was a necessary condition of the persistence of a housing boom over a cyclical depression.

Thus, besides the domestic factors discussed in an earlier section, there were foreign influences tending to inhibit building during the expansion phase of the trade cycle and encourage it during the depression phase. They may be summarized as follows:

(*a*) In the early nineteenth century people went to the towns when business was booming there, and stayed in the countryside or emigrated in slumps: that is, internal migration was dominated by the fluctuations in United Kingdom prosperity. But in the later part of the nineteenth century, internal migration was influenced by emigration, that is, by fluctuations in the prosperity of the regions of recent settlement. Costs of emigration had fallen, particularly in relation to the incomes of the potential migrants, and this tended to decrease the proportion of migration to the towns which took place during the trade-cycle expansion.

(*b*) The primary producing regions accentuated the shortage of funds available to the British building industry during the trade-cycle boom, by borrowing sums which in relation to contemporary British domestic investment were much larger than in the first half of the century, and by borrowing on securities more directly comparable and competitive with housing finance than were the securities of British industry.

The problem posed by the hypothesis of the Atlantic economy is the balance between domestic – and in this context fortuitous – influences on the one hand, and foreign and systematic influences on the other. The first long wave of British building in the 1870s is best interpreted as the result of domestic influences. Cooney has argued that the heavy foreign investment during the trade-cycle boom of 1869–73 diverted funds from building and in this way thrust the period of heavy building forward into the mid-seventies.[1] His argument seems to exaggerate the decline of building during this boom; with the principal exceptions of London and South Wales, housing activity rose fairly continuously from 1866 to 1876 with only a slight check in 1873. While it may be true that there would have been more building between 1869 and 1873 had it not been for the foreign demand for funds, I am inclined to think that the continued rise in building up to 1876 is principally to be explained by the fact that the trade-cycle boom did not come to an end in England with a financial panic, and that industrial activity remained at a high level even after 1873. These facts were not, of course, independent of events abroad, but they were not related in the direct way implied in the argument about systematic alternation.

But if British building had continued to repeat its pattern of the 1870s, it would have risen in the revival and continued on into the depression like every other trade cycle, and there would have been a partial overlapping instead of an inverse relationship. This is not what happened; the British building boom missed not one but two trade cycles. There was, it is true, an increase in building in the trade revival of the later eighties but there was no boom. There was indeed no general building boom between 1876, which saw the end of one, and 1896, which saw the beginning of another – a longer swing in fact than twenty years.

[1] E. W. Cooney, 'Long Waves in Building in the British Economy of the Nineteenth Century', *Economic History Review*, Second Series, XIII, No. 2 (December 1960), 264–6.

It is conceivable that a British building boom failed to develop in the late eighties because of the character of the industrial investment most prominent in the trade revival of those years. This was a revival after a very severe depression, concentrated mainly in exports and in the shipbuilding industry. There was a good deal of slack in the areas where the industries mainly concerned were situated, and a substantial increase in output and employment could take place with a relatively modest increase in internal migration.

But the main explanation is likely to have been the effect of the overseas development booms of these years. The 1880s are in many ways an exceptional decade. Foreign investment and emigration were sustained at a high level for a longer period than at any other time in the century. The cause of this is reasonably clear. Up to the 1870s by far the greater demand from regions of recent settlement for British migrants and funds had come from the United States. In the later 1870s and 1880s a sizeable demand arose from Australasia. The development booms did not coincide in all parts of Australasia, nor did Australasia coincide with the United States. There was also a large demand from South America. Whereas the overseas demand for finance and for migrants had previously tended to a considerable degree to be concentrated in the trade-cycle boom, it was now sustained for a decade and was, in addition, unusually heavy during the boom. It was so strong that, while not preventing the cyclical revival of the later 1880s in Britain, it drew off the migrants and/or funds which would have sustained a simultaneous boom in British building. This is the only occasion on which foreign influences clearly deflected British building fluctuations from the course they would otherwise have taken.

As between migrants and funds, it is unlikely that this deflection was produced by the outward flow of the latter.[1]

---

[1] Detailed comparison with German building fluctuations might shed light on the relative importance of migrants and funds. German foreign investment and exports went principally to Europe, and German emigrants went principally to America, and went during American booms; if the German building cycle had been determined by migration it ought, Lewis and O'Leary have argued, to have synchronized with the British. Instead, they believe it virtually coincided with

For this was a decade of low interest rates – consols were converted from 3 per cent to 2¾ per cent in 1888 – and funds were pushed abroad rather than pulled. The experience of the building societies does not suggest shortage of funds: at times during the eighties the directors of the Abbey Road Society were compelled to suspend the issue of shares because of the superabundance of money seeking investment.[1] In this decade the case for the importance of foreign influences must rest on emigration. Even in this decade the magnitude of emigration was in considerable measure the result of domestic influences. It is not merely that overseas areas were pulling migrants; English agriculture was pushing and English industry was not pulling hard enough. A large-scale migration from the English countryside was by then inevitable – by the later 1880s it was difficult to interpret the agricultural depression as the result of temporary circumstances. It is probable, too, that the depth of cyclical depression in 1879 and 1885 and the weakness of the intervening revival had made many industrial workers decide to emigrate, and that they acted on their decision as soon as the improvement of conditions provided them with the means to do so. But if certain regions of recent settlement had not been booming in this decade, more agricultural labourers would have gone to the English towns, and more urban workers would have stayed with them. This is the clearest case of emigration at the expense of urbanization.

---

the U.S. building cycle, with peaks in 1863 and 1890 ('Secular Swings in Production', p. 130), and with periods of heavy German capital exports (p. 142). But this does not shed much light on the problem because (a) German emigration was very much smaller in relation to total German population and did not necessarily bear the same relation to migration within Germany; (b) the evidence is, in fact, too slight to assert that the German building cycle coincided with the British.

[1] Sir Harold Bellman, *Bricks and Mortals* (London: Hutchinson & Co., 1949), pp. 66–7. The accounts of building societies are difficult to interpret because (a) each society was subject to individual influences; (b) the movement as a whole was affected by the failure of the Liberator Society (1892) and the Birkbeck (1911). Such as it is, the experience of the Abbey Road and the Co-operative Permanent suggests that the fluctuations in demand were much more important than those in funds. Certainly in periods of trade depression, for example 1885–6 and 1893–5, advances fell while receipts often rose. (A. Mansbridge, *Brick Upon Brick* (London: Dent & Sons, 1934), pp. 62–8.)

Once the fluctuations had been deflected from their former pattern, there was no reason why they should revert, even in the absence of further disturbance from abroad; indeed, on the view I have taken, there was every reason why the former pattern should *not* re-establish itself. One would expect the deficient building of the later 1880s to have produced a strong echo effect; so that even if there had been no subsequent fluctuations in foreign competition for funds and migrants after the eighties, building would probably have been high in the 1890s. If, as a result of events abroad in the second half of the eighties, the house-building of these years was unduly low, even for the level of demand in that decade, there would have been a backlog to be made up in the 1890s over and above houses for the migrants who in that decade turned away from the United States to English towns.

It is true that the extreme discredit which overtook foreign investment after the Australian and South American financial crises in the early nineties enhanced the attractions of domestic building mortgages to the passive investor; abundance of funds actively seeking such outlets allowed the building boom of the nineties to develop on a larger scale than might otherwise have been the case. But in the housing boom of the 1890s the contemporary influences which were most important were domestic. In this decade there was a change from industrial booms based on established industries to those based on new industries. Many of these developed in areas where there was no substantial surplus of labour at the beginning of the revival and where growth therefore stimulated considerable internal migration. As Charles Booth said in evidence before the London Transport Commission:

> The new industries that are started are not started in towns; they are started outside. I think anyone who travels through England cannot but notice the large new works that have been built in recent years and are being built near important stations, or still more near important junctions ... the development of trade at present is largely taking that shape. It is not so much that they are going out of the

towns, but they are not coming into the towns. But it must tend to move the population to a great extent; in fact, you see the houses of the working people being erected near these great new factories.[1]

Thus the character of the industries most prominent in the cycle was favourable to house-building.

It was in the nineties, moreover, that electricity was applied to transport in England with a resultant stimulus to suburban building. This illustrates better than anything else the random element in the relations of British and American building cycles. In the United States, electricity began to be applied to traction in the 1880s, and this had been one of the causes of the high level of American house-building in the eighties. If Britain had made similar advances in electricity in the 1880s she would have had a more substantial building boom in that decade. Thus the alternation of American and British housing activity in the eighties and nineties partly reflects the different rate at which electricity was applied to traction in the two countries. This was, in the present context, almost certainly fortuitous. It is, of course, true that if emigration from the United Kingdom in the 1880s had been smaller, urban authorities would have had more incentive to undertake improvements in local transport facilities. But the English lag in using electricity for this purpose was part of the lag in her use of electricity for all purposes, and this has nothing to do with the volume of migration to the United States and the heavy foreign investment during the 1880s. It was primarily the result of the relative efficiency of the English gas industry, and the unfortunate history of the electrical companies founded in the trade revival of the early eighties.

After 1903 there was a decline in building over the country as a whole, but as S. B. Saul has shown, this fall in the national total covers considerable diversity of regional experience.[2] Building was well sustained not only in the main centres of the

[1] R. C. on London Transport (Cd. 2751 of 1906, Qu. 19104, evidence given in March 1904).

[2] S. B. Saul, 'English Building Fluctuations in the 1890s', to appear in a forthcoming issue of *Economic History Review*.

export boom of this decade – in the coal fields of South Wales and Yorkshire, in the Lancashire cotton towns and in Liverpool – but in the East Midlands, which had been one of the main seats of engineering in the boom of the later nineties and where industry continued to expand. It is possible that where building was low it was because emigration depressed the demand for housing, and foreign investment depleted the funds. The main influence on internal migration, however, was not the level of emigration, but changes in the distribution of British industry, and where building declined after 1903 there is no evidence that it was because funds were diverted abroad. Except where demand was sustained by the continued growth of new industries or by the boom in exports, a decline in building was to be expected after 1903 simply because the previous housing boom had been so vigorous. There is no need to invoke foreign influences, and if they are invoked it can be argued that the demand of the primary producing regions for English goods in these years did more to stimulate building in England than their demand for migrants and funds did to depress it. It was only in the years immediately before 1914 that there were complaints that foreign investment was inhibiting British building, and the outbreak of war came too soon to enable us to judge how effective this competition for funds would ultimately have been in preventing the building revival which, from previous history, one would have expected in the second decade of the twentieth century.[1]

As an instance of the importance of not merely domestic but local influences on fluctuations, I take the case of London – exceptional in many ways, no doubt, but important since it has considerable influence on the behaviour of the national aggregate. In London there was a decline in building after 1903, which at first sight it might seem natural to attribute to foreign influences. But the fall can be accounted for by local circumstances. In the first place, London industries were

[1] For evidence of a shift from housing to foreign investment in the 1910s see *Report of the Land Enquiry Committee*, II (London, 1914). It was, of course, not only foreign investment which competed with housing but, for example, small joint-stock companies in textiles. (*Ibid.*, pp. 89–91.)

principally consumer industries, and these were not expanding rapidly in the decade or so before 1914 because real wages were stationary.[1] There is a link here with events abroad – the favourable terms of trade for primary products which partly accounted for the stagnation of real wages. But the link was indirect. The attractions of London as an industrial centre – mainly a large supply of cheap and diversified labour – were increasingly offset by the rising price of sites within the central area.[2] While one effect of this was to induce factories to move from central London to outlying areas, possibly increasing the demand for houses there, it must have deterred new manufacturers coming to London and impaired the competitive power of London manufacturers against those of less densely populated areas.

Building in London had been unusually active in the 1870s, stimulated by the development of the horse tramway – the peak of building was not reached in London till 1881. There was in these years a large amount of building in Camberwell, Walworth, Forest Hill, Stamford, and Tottenham, much of it associated with improved transport facilities.[3] The Great Eastern Railway, whose London stations were in the crowded parts of the East End, ran cheap workmen's trains, under statutory obligation, from the mid-1870s.[4] There was a large amount of speculative building of working-class houses. The building boom of the 1870s was therefore more prolonged in London than almost anywhere else. Some of the activity in the London building boom of the later 1890s was in areas where there had already been very considerable building as recently as 1881, Tottenham, for example, and it might for this reason be expected to peter out earlier.[5]

---

[1] Between 1901–11, there was a net emigration from the Greater London area of 228,733. J. C. Spensley, 'Urban Housing Problems', *Journal of the Royal Statistical Society*, LXXXI, Pt. II (March 1918), 173.

[2] R. C. on London Traffic, Cd. 2597 of 1905, Qu. 21651 ff., 21678.

[3] R. C. on Housing of the Working Classes, P.P. 1881, VI, Qu. 3987.

[4] Ibid., P. P. 1881, VII, Qu. 1444.

[5] There was probably also a long-standing tendency for London building to be out of phase with that of industrial areas. Thus the 1830s seem to have seen less building in London than in the rest of the country – between 1831 and 1841 the number of inhabited houses per hundred of population rose over the country

Then again, a large part of the building in this boom of the later 1890s was in places where transport facilities were already available. 'The enormous migration of people into Tottenham, Edmonton, West Ham, and Walthamstow and such districts,' said one witness before the Commission on London Transport of 1905, 'is simply caused by the facilities that have been given by the railway companies.'[1] It was the provision of cheap workmen's trains running out considerable distances that was said to be the most important cause of the exceptionally rapid growth of population in the districts of London adjacent to the suburbs.[2] It was cheap trains which had caused the increase in population, not vice versa. This was a type of business which the railway representatives before the Commission made it clear they disliked. Its concentration at peak hours would in itself – quite apart from the limit on fares – have made it uneconomic, and cheap workmen's fares, by changing the social composition of the suburbs to which they were available, tended to reduce the more profitable types of traffic. There were also special difficulties in London in building new suburban lines – mainly the high cost of land and the difficulty of acquiring it, and there were particular difficulties in the provision of tramways.

Thus the fluctuations in London building are partly to be explained by independently determined changes in the provision of cheap travelling facilities. The explanation of the relatively low level of London building after 1903 is not simply that demand for housing was growing less rapidly in London than elsewhere. There is a large amount of evidence given before the Royal Commission on Means of Locomotion and Transport in London which suggests that there was still in 1904 a large unsatisfied demand for housing in London. The cost of land and the high rates made it virtually impossible to

---

as a whole, but fell in Middlesex (Matthews, *A Study in Trade-Cycle History*, p. 118). This disparity of experience may have had some echo effect in later decades. It also suggests the possibility that migration into London tended to vary inversely with the prosperity of the industrial districts.

[1] Cd. 2597 to 1905, Qu. 2751, 3799.
[2] Ibid., Qu. 5058.

build profitably in any central district.[1] Commercial builders would not build around London until means of access at cheap rates were assured. Building therefore depended on the creation of cheap suburban transport, and this was slow for reasons which have little to do with events abroad, for example, the fact that suburban fares were too low, and the limited capacity of the London stations.

That very local factors had an important effect on fluctuations is not of course a demonstration that the systematic influence was not the crucial variable. But the study of a particular area does reinforce one's scepticism.

The argument of this essay is not that emigration and foreign investment had no effect on British building fluctuations, but only that except in the later eighties they were of minor importance compared with domestic factors. These foreign influences were of such a nature that they *could* have dominated British building, but it is only in the later eighties that it may reasonably be supposed that foreign influences did in fact deflect it from the path dictated by its previous history and by contemporary developments of a primarily domestic origin. The argument has been confined to the influence on British fluctuations of the overseas demand for British funds and migrants, because this seems the direction in which effects hypothesized by the theory of the Atlantic economy are most likely to have worked. But it would of course be equally a verification of the theory if an exceptionally strong British demand for funds and migrants called a temporary halt to growth in the overseas regions; it has indeed been argued that the British boom of the later 1980s inhibited the flow of capital and labour to Canada and held up a revival which was warranted by purely Canadian conditions.[2] This part of the

[1] R. C. on London Traffic, Cd. 2751 of 1906, Qu. 5799, 5908. This is also related to the social structure of London. A very large proportion of London's industrial labour was employed in domestic industry – in the small workshop. There was, therefore, more residence near place of work than in factory towns. Moreover, though there was a class of prosperous artisans, the mass of London's domestic workers enjoyed lower earnings than factory workers. They could less easily afford the economic cost of travel from the suburbs.

[2] K. A. H. Buckley, *Capital Formation in Canada, 1896–1930* (Toronto; University of Toronto Press, 1955).

argument must be left to transatlantic historians, but since the overseas economies were growing more rapidly than the British and their cyclical booms were more vigorous, I should expect to find the autonomous element in their fluctuations even more evident than in the British.

6 Capital Imports and the Composition of Investment in a Borrowing Country

A. R. HALL

[This article was first published in A. R. Hall, *The London Capital Market and Australia, 1870–1914*, Australian National University Press, 1963.]

There are two conclusions of Roland Wilson's *Capital Imports and the Terms of Trade* the implications of which have not been fully appreciated by Australian economic historians (including the present writer a dozen years ago) and perhaps by economic theorists in general. They are first 'the probability that "domestic" prices will in general rise relatively to import and export prices in the borrowing country', and second 'that some verification is found in Australian experience for the proposition that imports of capital *tend* to be positively correlated with increases in the ratio of the "domestic" price level to the price level of "international" commodities'.[1] The implications are that such a shift in relative prices ought to be reflected in relative profitability. To the extent that this is so then there should also be a relative shift in investment towards the production of 'domestic' or 'non-traded' goods.

The way in which this process may be expected to work itself out can be described along these lines.[2] The central assumptions from which we begin are: that the borrowing country is small in relation to its export markets and in terms of its suppliers of imports; that at the outset it has a comparative advantage in land; and that for convenience it produces and spends on two

[1] Roland Wilson, op. cit., pp. 81 and 106. Italics in the original. Both conclusions are well hedged with qualifications.

[2] I am indebted to T. W. Swan for assistance in formulating this argument. It does not necessarily, however, reflect his views.

types of goods – traded goods (exportables and importables) and non-traded goods.

Initially it is assumed that the borrowing country is not fully employed either in terms of labour or capacity except in the field of capacity for producing exports. Its comparative advantage in (pastoral) exports is not fully exploited. It borrows abroad in order to further exploit these resources. The accompanying act of investment will have the normal Keynesian expansionary effects. It will also have multiplier effects in a different sense. If, for example, expenditure is normally equally divided between traded and non-traded goods then the initial investment will only effect a reduction in the trade balance equal to half the original investment in which case only half the original import of capital will have been transferred. On the assumption of no transfer of gold, another round of expenditure will be necessary for the full capital import to have been achieved through changes in the trade balance. That this is so depends partly on the assumption that there will be no short period terms of trade effect necessarily involved in the process of making the capital transfer. This is axiomatic if the country concerned is small in relation to its market for exports and supply of imports for under these conditions its export and import prices are determined abroad. Even if it were of the same size there would still be no presumption that the terms of trade would necessarily move in either direction in order to effect the capital transfer.

Partly because the process of investment takes time to be completed the expansion induced by an initial decision to invest, which is financed from abroad, has greater stimulating effects than one which is financed from local savings. Thus the initial act of raising funds from abroad will add to the liquidity of the borrowing country until such time as the funds are transferred through the appropriate movement in the trade balance. Under competitive conditions the increase in liquidity would tend to lower interest rates in the borrowing country. In doing so it would provide some stimulus to other domestic investment, especially for investment in long-lived assets. Whether such investment was in fact stimulated would depend on the degree and industrial distribution of the excess capacity which was initially assumed to be present. Apart from the effects of possible interest rate changes, and probably of greater importance account should also be taken of the process of credit creation through a domestic banking system whose lending actions were influenced by changes in the level of London funds.[1]

If the act of foreign financed investment were of a once and for all character then the expansionary processes would soon be reversed. If it represented the appearance of a new level of capital inflow the multiplier effects would work themselves out over time until a new equilibrium had been established. If the rate of capital inflow continued to increase there would be a cumulative expansion of investment and output in the borrowing country.

In the last mentioned case sooner or later there would be a rise in the price of non-traded goods relative to traded goods or, in the context of the 1880s, their prices would fall more slowly than would those of traded goods. This would be so because for the time being the assumption is being maintained that export and import prices continue to be determined abroad. There is, however, no such limitation on the prices of non-traded goods. As there was a progressive shift into full capacity in non-traded goods their prices would begin to rise. This would improve the relative profit prospects in industries producing non-traded goods.[2] In so far as one of the prices tending to rise was that of labour it would simultaneously tend to reduce the profit prospects of industries producing traded goods which would be in no position to counter rising costs by raising their prices.

If inflows of labour occurred simultaneously with the inflow of capital then the process of expansion could occur unhindered by the appearance of bottlenecks in the supply of labour.

---

[1] Compare S. J. Butlin, *Australia and New Zealand Bank* (Melbourne 1961), p. 121.

[2] In so far as there was a price rise for importables, absorbed in the profits of importers rather than reflected in import prices, there would also be a stimulus for import competing industries.

Inflows of labour would, however, serve to minimize or eliminate rises in its price so that this aspect of the shift in relative profitability in favour of non-traded goods might not emerge or be very strong. If the process of expansion continued until full employment of labour and capacity was reached then a situation would arise in which the switch of resources into non-traded goods production would be accentuated by a general rise of their prices relative to those of traded goods.

This whole process is not, however, self-perpetuating. The reverse is in fact the case. Sooner or later the process of investment in the original autonomous field of comparative advantage will come to an end as the subsequent increases in output progressively reduce the initial profitability of investment in that field. Here it becomes necessary to relax the assumption of unchanged terms of trade. Even if the borrowing country initially was a small supplier of its main export, e.g. wool, a sustained process of investment of the type envisaged, given its comparative advantage, would result in a situation in which it became a relatively large supplier of that export in which case the price of the export is no longer simply dependent on conditions abroad but on the supply of exports from the borrowing country. The result of the investment process would therefore tend to be a long-term adverse movement in the terms of trade of the borrowing country. This alone would tend to bring the process of investment in that export industry to an end.

A reduction of profitability in the initial field of investment might not, however, of itself bring the process of capital importing to an end. The profit opportunities generated by the relative shift of prices in favour of non-traded goods (building in particular) might be sufficient in themselves to act as a magnet for further capital inflows. But here again sooner or later the investment prospects would be exploited, though in this field in particular the timing of their exhaustion may be concealed by the speculative activity likely to develop in the final stages of a building boom and by the frantic efforts of those concerned with urban finance to uphold an increasingly unstable structure of property values.

As an aside to the main argument it should perhaps be pointed out that it may be argued that the building boom of the 1880s was a consequence of elements other than the shift in relative profitability consequent upon the rate of growth of capital inflow. In particular it may be argued that it was partly a consequence of urbanization. More recently it has become apparent that it was partly a consequence of the highly skewed age distribution of the Victorian and N.S.W. populations in 1881 which was of a character likely to induce a rapid rate of growth of demand for housing during the next decade in the absence of capital inflows.

With regard to the first point there are good reasons for believing that urbanization was an integral part of the whole process. Thus if the autonomous element is investment in land (wool in Australia, beef in the Argentine, wheat in Canada); if the consequential process of production from land is not of a labour intensive character; and if there are simultaneous inflows of labour and capital; then the technical conditions are likely to be such that urbanization is an inevitable consequence.

For the purposes of the present argument the skewed age distribution of the population of Australia and especially Victoria in 1881 must be regarded as an independent factor. It was the delayed effect, in terms of housing demand, of the rapid growth of births at the end of the 1850s. This in turn was a consequence of the population 'explosion' which was one aspect of the gold rushes of the 1850s. Theorists of long waves might wish to incorporate this movement into an integrated analysis of long period international flows of capital and labour. To our mind the Australian story is merely the working out of a once and for all major shock to the age structure of the population. The wave-like movement over time of this major kink in the age structure which has continued to the present day has sometimes been dampened and sometimes exaggerated by changing economic conditions.[1]

[1] For a more detailed discussion of the changes in the age composition of the Australian population and their effects on economic events see the writer's article 'Some Long Period Effects of the Kinked Age Distribution of the Population of Australia 1861–1961', *Economic Record*, March 1963.

Whether or not one wishes to incorporate all these processes into one integrated causal sequence is, however, irrelevant for the present argument. It is sufficient merely to show that it is likely that over time the main demand for oversea capital will switch from investment in exports to investment in non-traded goods and that in the Australian context of the 1880s such a process was made even more likely by the growth of urbanization and the skewed age distribution of the population.

To return to the main theme. The point had been reached where investment opportunities in land had been temporarily exploited and where it would only be a matter of time before this was also true for investment in buildings. In this situation it becomes increasingly probable that the process will be brought to an end by a change in the rate of supply of foreign funds. The longer the period during which the rate of capital inflow has increased to one particular borrower, the larger it is likely to be relatively as well as absolutely and the more is it likely to place strains on the lending capacity of the supplier of funds. If there are other potential borrowers who have not received capital inflows to the same extent as the borrowing country being examined, then the probability that their demand for funds will grow relative to that borrower increases as it becomes more and more likely that their comparative advantages are not exploited to a comparable extent. It is only necessary that this growing competition for available funds should produce a cessation of the rate of growth of lending to the original borrower for the expansionary process to come to an end as the stimulating influence of the capital inflow lies in its rate of increase.

So long as the rate of capital inflow is increasing the relative diversion of resources into non-traded industry is unlikely by itself to create balance of payments difficulties. Once the rate of capital inflow levels off, however, there will be a period during which earlier multiplier effects will be operating and in which there will still be a relative shift of resources into non-traded goods without corresponding accruals of foreign exchange. At this time the process of diverting resources into non-traded goods will produce pressure on the balance of payments. If there are simultaneous increasingly unfavourable movements in the terms of trade then the situation is obviously growing untenable at a rapid rate. It would reach a crisis state without outside intervention but in practice the crisis is likely to be brought on by some event which is accidental in terms of the logic of the processes being discussed. Thus while, there are clear signs of the process coming to an end in Australia before 1890 it was the Baring crisis, which in a sense was independent of conditions in Australia, that hastened the drawing to an end of the long phase of foreign financed investment in Australia.

This outline theory of the effects of capital inflow on the changing composition of investment in the borrowing country is obviously incomplete. It is difficult to believe, however, that it will not stand up to the test of rigorous theoretical formulation. That this is so is confirmed, to the extent that economic theory is ever confirmed by practice, by its obvious good fit with the sequence of events in later nineteenth-century Australia. Readers of Chapter V will be aware that it was not informed by this particular theoretical viewpoint. In some places in fact it calls for a change in emphasis, but for the most part it serves to tighten the logic of that analysis. In particular it explains in a way that was hitherto not very satisfactory the increasing diversion of resources into the building industry in the 1880s and gives added point to the analysis of the effects of changes in the rate of supply of British capital on the level of economic activity in Australia.

While the theory was developed with the specific experience of Australia in mind it may, of course, be generalized to include other areas of recent settlement. In a world economy in which new sources of land were progressively being brought into the world market partly as a result of the technical consequences of the invention of railways and steamships it was inevitable that these new areas would have a comparative advantage in one or other of the many possible uses of new land. In a world in which some areas, and one in particular, had relatively excess supplies of capital it was natural for part of that capital to move abroad in order to take advantage of the new comparative advantages in land (used in a sense to include minerals).

The stimulating effects of an increase in the rate of capital inflow on the borrowing country would not be limited to the export industries. A general expansion of investment would follow. If the process continued for any length of time, and the increase in the rate of capital inflow was in itself likely to have such an effect, then increasingly one could expect a relative shift in investment in favour of non-traded goods, in particular into the building industry. This was even more likely if there were large simultaneous inflows of labour and if the technical nature of land exploitation were such that it was not particularly labour intensive. The association of large-scale capital inflows with large-scale building booms thus becomes inevitable and the apparent paradox of capital inflows directed at the exploitation of comparative advantages in land becoming capital inflows directed at the exploitation of non-traded goods is no paradox at all but merely part of the normal sequence of events.

When there were more than one new areas of land being opened up and when there were obviously a variety of ways in which land could be utilized it was inevitable that not all new areas were likely to have the same comparative advantage at the same time. Similarly the strength of the derived fluctuations in building would vary with the relative rates of inflow of labour and with the technical conditions under which it was employed. While the common source of funds, the London capital market, would help to keep these movements in phase the relative amplitude of the fluctuations would vary at different times in the same country and between different countries at the same time. Thus there is, in principle, no reason to be surprised that the particular process of exploiting wool in Australia gave it a peculiar eminence in the 1870s and 1880s while it was out of the mainstream of international capital flows in the early twentieth century when it was Canada's wheat frontier which probably gave it pride of place in London's eyes.

Viewed in terms of this worldwide process of exploiting particular comparative advantages the narrowing of the difference in output per head between Australia and the United

Kingdom that has recently been detected by N. G. Butlin falls naturally into place. At about 1860 a high rate of productivity in Australia would largely represent a large marginal contribution from land (gold and wool). The natural effect of the exhaustion of easily exploited gold and of the process of investment in the pastoral industry would be to reduce the marginal product of land. In addition the progressive switch of investment into non-traded goods meant that the relative share in gross national production of the high productivity land industries would decline. In the industries which were absorbing an increasing share of Australia's resources one would not expect the marginal production of labour in Australia to be higher than that in the United Kingdom. If anything it would be less. In the long term in a world economy in which there were more or less free flows of capital and labour directed towards the exploitation of regional comparative advantages it is to be expected that there would be a narrowing of international differences in output per head.

There are two corollaries of this view of international capital flows and of Australian experience in particular that may be worth mentioning. The second of these is a particular application of the first. This is that it is misleading as has sometimes been the case among Australian economic historians to regard Australia's economic destiny to have been largely shaped within Australia. If one's gaze is concentrated upon the Australian scene this will almost inevitably be the judgement of the historian. It will be Australians who see market opportunities, borrow capital to exploit them; and bring about their own downfall. If, however, one stands back from the scene it becomes increasingly clear that some of the most important market opportunities are shaped by conditions abroad; that the availability of oversea capital is dependent upon conditions other than in Australia; and that the downfall may be a consequence of the working out of changes which occurred abroad a year or two earlier. There is truth in both points of view. What is wrong is to regard one as exclusive of the other.

The particular application of this rule is that it is wrong to discuss the story of British capital inflow simply in terms of the initiative of Australian borrowers and conversely to regard the activity of British investors as passive. As has been argued at length the passiveness implied in saying 'yes' to an inveterate borrower must sooner or later be converted into a positive 'no'. That 'no' was said in the early 1890s and even, perhaps, in the more important sense of 'no greater rate' in the middle 1880s is not the crucial point. What is crucial is that the very fact of British capital inflow helped to shape the conditions under which Australian entrepreneurs exercised their initiative. As this was so it becomes a pointless hen and egg problem to bestow the initiative on any one set of participants. The only fruitful way to view the process or British capital inflow to Australia is to regard it as one of interaction between conditions in Australia and in Britain.

7 Investment in Canada, 1900–13

A. K. CAIRNCROSS

[This article was first published in A. K. Cairncross, *Home and Foreign Investment 1870–1913*, Cambridge University Press, 1953.]

This essay starts from a very simple point, but one which, in previous discussions of investment in Canada, has hardly received the attention which it deserves. Investment by one country in another means a transfer, not of purchasing power in the sense either of cash or of income, but of capital. Changes in the money supply and in incomes may accompany a transfer of capital: but they are plainly not the same thing. A transfer of capital (at any rate where capital is being borrowed for productive investment) means that one country's stock of instruments of production is enlarged out of the savings of another country. It means, as a rule, that certain changes take place in employment and constructional activity in both countries; that, for example, the borrowing country experiences a building boom while the building trade in the lending country is depressed. These are the fundamental changes. And we must never be led to neglect them by concentration on monetary changes and banking policies.

I *The Background to Investment*

Investment in Canada after 1900 took place against a background of scarcity and expansion. First, and above all, there was an almost continual scarcity of labour. Complaints of labour shortage came from all lines of business. In manufacturing, employers reported that they were ready and anxious to employ many more hands if suitable men could be found.

Railway construction was repeatedly held up while contractors searched for men; sometimes horses stood idle in the stables because teamsters were unobtainable. At harvest time the shortage was acute; the railway companies undertook the transport of labour from the east, and special arrangements were made to bring labourers from abroad with a view to settlement of the immigrants out of their harvest earnings. In mines and lumber camps, in building, domestic service and transportation, the same scarcity of labour was everywhere felt.

There was a shortage, secondly, of concrete capital. The rapid growth of population and the immigration of large numbers of young workers strained the limited supply of house-room to the point of famine. Between 1901 and 1911 the number of occupied dwelling houses increased by 387,000, in the same period the number of families increased by 447,000.[1] The shortage was greatest in the western provinces. At Calgary, for example, 'scores of citizens' had to keep their families in the east because there were no houses to be had. In British Columbia, more than a quarter of the married men had left their wives in some other province or country, presumably for the same reason.

Congestion on the railways was almost equally great. After every abundant harvest there was a shortage of cars. In the summer, the companies were hard put to it at times to arrange for the transport of settlers and their effects. New track and equipment were constantly required for homesteads, mines, and lumber camps off the existing railway routes; and the additional traffic carried on these new branch lines made it necessary to provide larger terminals and repair shops.

The scarcity of these and other forms of concrete capital expressed itself in a corresponding scarcity of money capital. If the country was to be opened up rapidly, an enormous outlay on the purchase or construction of capital instruments was essential. To meet this outlay the savings of Canadians

---

[1] In the previous decade both increased by only 150,000. The number of persons per dwelling rose from 5·2 in 1901 to 5·9 in 1911, although the average size of family fell simultaneously.

were altogether inadequate. There was not enough capital inside Canada. Canadian savings had to be supplemented, therefore, by borrowings from abroad. The size of the borrowings which Canada succeeded in making is some measure of the scarcity of capital after 1900.

Scarcity in all these forms led not unnaturally to higher costs. Weekly wages, to deal first with labour, rose by nearly 50 per cent, and hourly rates in an even higher ratio.[1] The rise varied enormously between localities and industries, so that we cannot speak of average changes with much confidence. Some broad conclusions would appear, however, to be warranted by the evidence. First of all, there was a rise in real wages as well as in money wages. The cost of living increased by from 40 to 45 per cent, while weekly wage-rates increased by nearly 50 per cent.[2] Secondly, the rise in wages was greatest in the sheltered industries and least in those which had to face competition from imports. In building, domestic service, printing, transportation, and municipal service, the average increase was 58 per cent;[3] in mining, brewing, and the leather, textile, and metal industries the average increase was 31·5 per cent, or, if the clothing trades (including tailoring, etc.) are included, by 37 per cent.[4] In agriculture the rise was intermediate – just over 50 per cent.[5] Thirdly, the changes in wages and prices in differ-

[1] The reduction in hours between 1900 and 1913 was probably about 5 per cent on the average (cf. the data in the *Cost of Living Report*, Vol. II, p. 431).

[2] Up to 1910 weekly wage-rates and the cost of living kept pace with one another, and even in 1912 the indices given in Table V (below p. 180) show only a 1 per cent difference. The index of weekly wages used by Viner (*Canada's Balance of International Indebtedness, 1900–13*, p. 243), and taken from the *Cost of Living Report* shows a slightly faster rise in money wages up to 1912 and a gradual rise in real wages.

[3] Calculated from data in the *Cost of Living Report*, Vol. II, pp. 428–30. The weights given by Coats (building 14; domestic service, 20, printing, 2; transportation, 8, municipal service, ½) have been used.

[4] Calculated from data cited above. The weights used were: mining, 5; brewing and distilling, ½; leather, 1; textiles, 3; metals, 8; clothing, 7.

[5] These figures are for weekly earnings. They are based upon quotations that did not remain constant in number, and to which the chain method appears not to have been applied. No serious error, however, is involved. In the building industry, where hours were reduced by about 9 per cent, the rise in hourly rates of wages varied from 52 per cent (bricklayers) to 90 per cent (rough carpenters), and averaged 70 per cent. In no other industry did hours fall so heavily.

ent provinces were such as to raise real wages faster in the west than in the east. Generally speaking, the further west the province the higher, both in 1900 and in 1913, were money wages and the cost of living. But between 1900 and 1913 there was a levelling up in wages and prices, both rising faster in the east than in the west. As the levelling-up process was carried further in prices than in wages, the result was a relative improvement in real wages in the provinces west of Ontario. But the change in favour of the west – especially when rents are taken into account – was not great.

Scarcity of concrete capital did not lead everywhere to a rise in the price which its services fetched. The rent of dwelling-houses, it is true, increased by from 60 to 70 per cent, and business rents increased twice as rapidly. But railway charges remained practically constant, freight rates moving down and passenger rates up. Public utility charges, too, were for the most part lower. The failure of these prices to rise can be explained in part by the large measure of public control exercised over them. Prices were regulated by statute, charter, or public commission, and were not determined solely by considerations of profit.[1] Nevertheless, the fact that public utilities continued to make large profits at the low prices is an indication that other factors were at work. Of these, one was obviously the coming into play of economies of scale. Whereas the provision of more house-room became progressively more expensive the faster the population grew, the provision of water, gas, electricity, and transport became progressively cheaper. Moreover, the fact that houses required to be built by Canadian labour, whereas rails, locomotives, generating equipment, tubes, boilers, and so on could be manufactured by foreign labour whose wages rose less rapidly, kept down costs in public utilities relatively to building costs.

The changes in the price structure are illustrated in Chart 1. They were not all by any means in the direction normal to inflation: wholesale prices lagged behind the cost of living, and the cost of living lagged slightly behind money wages. The fan opening out between import prices, export prices and

[1] Viner, op. cit., p. 245.

domestic prices each progressively more free to cut loose from the movement of world prices, does, however, exhibit the normal outcome of inflation in a country running up an adverse balance of payments.

Finally, scarcity of money capital sent up the rate of interest.

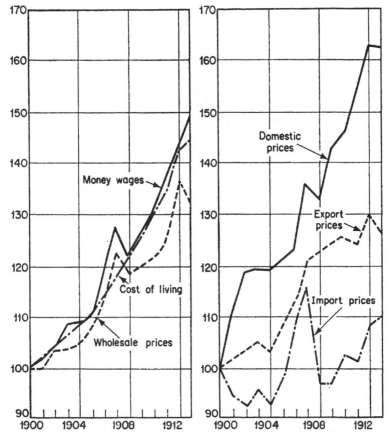

CHART I. (*a*) Wages and prices, 1900–13; (*b*) Import, export, and domestic prices, 1900–13.

The return both on Dominion and on Provincial government bonds rose by 20 per cent, on first mortgages on city house property in the same proportion, and on the bonds of cities, counties, and townships by upwards of 40 per cent. The terms on which Canada was able to borrow in London and New York grew steadily more onerous.

With scarcity and rising prices went expansion. In every year except 1908 and 1909, the labour supply was augmented by immigrants from Europe and the United States. On balance, about 650,000 persons, a large proportion of whom were young men in the prime of life, settled in Canada in the decade 1901–11. In the next three years, the net immigration was nearly 500,000, more than the natural increase of population in the same period.[1] On the average, for every two Canadians entering

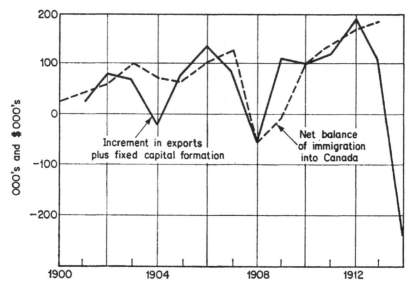

CHART 2. Immigration into Canada and economic expansion, 1900–13.

the labour market for the first time, three immigrants offered their services simultaneously.[2] Not only did immigration dominate the labour market in terms of magnitude; it dominated it also in sensitivity. So long as there was a shortage of labour, immigrants poured in; wherever the demand for

[1] These figures are almost certainly underestimates. There is reason to believe that net immigration in the decade 1901–11 was at least 1 million (see p. 184).

[2] The number of immigrant arrivals were 2,850,000, or 200,000 per annum. A small proportion, about 15 per cent, of these were children. On the average, therefore, about 170,000 persons entered the Canadian labour market annually; if we omit married women, perhaps 150,000 persons. At the same time, about 110,000 Canadian-born children reached the age of 15 in each year between 1905 and 1910. Of course, large numbers of immigrants and Canadians migrated later to the United States and other countries. But we are dealing here only with entrance to Canadian industry.

labour was deficient and no jobs were to be had, intending immigrants stayed where they were, while workers in Canada moved to countries less depressed or more congenial. The burden of adjustment to changing demands for labour was borne largely by migrants.

With expansion of the labour supply went investment in capital of all kinds. Roughly $2,500 million was borrowed abroad – not far short of Canada's own savings during the period – and out of the proceeds, railway tracks and towns were built, and lands, forests, and mines were developed, often with immigrant labour. The capital equipment (and the debt) of the country enormously increased.

The driving force behind Canadian development in those years was the rise in agricultural prices all over the world. From the mid-nineties onwards, Canadian exports were fetching higher and higher prices, while interest rates and construction costs remained comparatively low. Thus the scarcity of labour and of capital equipment in Canada were symptoms of a more fundamental scarcity of Canadian export goods on world markets.[1] Investment and immigration kept step with export prices.[2]

The large stretches of fertile prairie which the railways kept opening up enabled Canada to take increasing advantage of high prices without immediate risk of an equal rise in costs. High prices operated in conjunction with an elastic supply of virgin land; development was profitable and there was plenty of room for development. But it would be a mistake to lay stress exclusively on agricultural development. The rise in

---

[1] The price of grains and fodders at wholesale in Canada rose by 37·1 per cent between the triennial periods 1901–3 and 1911–13; animals and meats rose by 38·9 per cent; and dairy produce by 33·8 per cent. By contrast, the average rise in wholesale prices in Canada was only 21·6 per cent. (These estimates are based on the indices in the *Cost of Living Report*, Vol. II, p. 20.)

[2] It may be suggested that Canadian export prices had little to do with the decisions about railway-building taken by the Canadian Government (or even by the companies). But these decisions were taken in a boom atmosphere which was largely the product of high export prices; and the railway-building would have been much more costly (and probably much less rapid) had it not been for the confidence of the British investor in the healthy prospects of the primary Canadian industries.

F

export prices was not the sole factor at work. Between 1900 and 1913 rich deposits of mineral ores were found and developed in the Cobalt, Porcupine, and other districts. Canada became the leading nickel producer in the world, and copper, silver, and gold were exported in large quantities. These minerals sold at low prices, but mining costs were also low and production was highly profitable. In other industries, improved methods of production were favourable to an expansion in Canadian output.[1]

The process of expansion was thrice interrupted. About the autumn of 1903 there began a transient depression which lasted till the end of 1904 and was felt mainly in the east. A second and much more severe depression spread from the western provinces in the early summer of 1907 and continued all through 1908. The third and last depression, that of 1913–14, also began in the west.

II *Investment and the Balance of Payments*

We may now return to the thesis with which this essay began and analyse the connection between a transfer of capital to Canada and the volume of investment in Canada: that is, between investment and the balance of payments.

An increase in investment, unaccompanied by any change in thrift, tends to raise money incomes. An increase in exports generally has the same effect. The rise in incomes, initiated from the side of investment or of exports, tends to be cumulative. At first there may be some disinvestment of stocks, or some increase in short-term funds abroad. Later, as incomes continue to expand, savings are made and there is an increased outlay on imports. The original adjustments give place to others once the settled preferences of consumers find time to express themselves. But at each stage along the path of expansion one fundamental equation will be satisfied. We have:[2]

---

[1] Cf. Viner, op. cit., pp. 264–7.

[2] I abstain from precise definition in the hope that these terms are sufficiently intelligible without further explanation.

Investment in Canada ('Home Investment')

- = Borrowing from abroad + Canadian investment in Canada

- = Debit balance of payments on current account + Canadian investment abroad + Canadian investment in Canada

- = Imports − Exports + Canadian savings.

Hence

'Home Investment' + Exports = Canadian Savings + Imports.

This equation may be interpreted causally to mean that any increase in the joint total of home investment and exports will drive up income to a level at which Canadians seek to make an exactly equal addition to their savings and expenditure on imports. Such an interpretation, however, is possible only with important qualifications.

First of all, a *net* increase in home investment or in exports – and still more in the sum of the two – is frequently the balance of an initial increase at one point over the resultant decrease at another. A rise in railway-building may force up interest rates and check house-building; a rise in wheat exports may be achieved by creating a scarcity of labour in the lumber camps. Again, exports may go up because investment is falling; for instance, when credit restriction forces merchants to dispose of stocks abroad, or when unemployment and reduced buying power are freeing goods for export which, in better times, would find a market at home. Or exports may fall off because of an expansion in investment and home demand. A primary change in investment or in exports works through other forms of investment and other exports as well as through incomes, savings, and imports.

Secondly, savings and imports are not passive factors depending solely on income as determined by the current level of investment and export. A change in thrift may be of some importance, especially when prices alter so as to redistribute income in favour of the thrifty. A rise in import prices, by raising the cost of living, can also affect the demand for Canadian goods and so depress Canadian incomes. The public may seek to buy imports in preference to home-produced goods. And so on. Nevertheless, there is overwhelming evidence that, so long as incomes remain constant, outlay on consumable goods (home-produced and imported) is remarkably constant also, and that, in the short run, it is fluctuations in income which, more than anything else, alter savings and imports.[1] It is to home investment and exports, therefore, that we must look for an explanation of the changes that took place in the Canadian balance of payments.

It is not easy to test this reasoning against the facts. There are no statistical series for investment and savings, carefully defined. In 1937 I made a number of hazardous calculations in an article published in *Weltwirtschaftliches Archiv* (on which the present essay is based) and emerged with estimates which I labelled 'Canadian Home Investment' for the years 1900–13. It is unnecessary to reproduce these calculations here as they have now been superseded by the much more thorough investigations undertaken by Dr K. A. H. Buckley of the University of Saskatchewan.[2] Dr Buckley has been kind enough to allow me to make use of his estimates, which are given in Table I.

Dr Buckley's estimates are partly on an annual, partly on a quinquennial basis. The annual figures cover constructional activity (including repair work), and investment in machinery and equipment, but not changes in stocks. The quinquennial figures show new construction and repair separately and include estimates of the net change in stocks. Since the data do not permit of the estimation of annual changes in stocks, the best that can be done is to use fixed capital formation (gross of repairs) as an index of changes in home investment. Unfortunately, this makes it impossible to attach any precise

---

[1] Cf., for example, C. Bresciani-Turroni, 'Egypt's balance of payments', *J. Polit. Econ.* 1934; and J. H. Williams, *Argentine's International Balance of Indebtedness.*

[2] 'Real Investment in Canada, 1900 to 1930' (unpublished dissertation available in the London School of Economics Library).

meaning to the corresponding concept on the side of savings. I shall make use of the term 'Gross Canadian Savings', conscious that it will diverge from actual savings whenever the level of stocks is in course of change, and that it will exceed

TABLE I *Fixed Capital Formation in Canada, 1900–15*

Year	Value of total construction* ($m.)	Gross investment in machinery and equipment† ($m.)	Total fixed capital formation ($m.)	Net increase in inventories‡ ($m.)	Cost of construction § (1900–4 = 100)
1900	127	52	179		95·9
1901	127	60	187 ⎫		94·8
1902	156	73	229 ⎪		99·4
1903	194	90	284 ⎬	222	103·8
1904	213	75	288 ⎪		106·0
1905	247	82	329 ⎭		109·1
1906	307	100	407 ⎫		116·6
1907	351	125	476 ⎪		123·3
1908	316	108	424 ⎬	262	123·0
1909	383	117	500 ⎪		121·6
1910	440	136	576 ⎭		126·1
1911	519	167	686 ⎫		129·4
1912	586	224	810 ⎪		133·9
1913	580	249	829 ⎬	360	141·8
1914	471	170	641 ⎪		137·9
1915	355	102	457 ⎭		135·7

* K. A. H. Buckley, op. cit. p. 49. These figures include repairs estimated by Dr Buckley at $255 million for 1901–5, $403 million for 1906–10, and $523 million for 1911–15. The figures for 1912 have been amended by Dr Buckley.

† Ibid., pp. 90–3. I have added an allowance for freight and mark-ups on the basis of quinquennial estimates given by Dr Buckley.

‡ Ibid., p. 116.

§ Ibid., p. 49. I have converted from a 1913 to a 1900–4 base.

net savings by including both sums expended on repairs and sums required for the replacement of capital assets.

The most important constituent of gross home investment in Canada was undoubtedly railway-building. A further large item was the construction of highways, bridges, canals, and harbours. These two items together accounted in 1913 for nearly $300 million out of a total of just over $800 million.

Dr Buckley's estimates for this group – which falls a little short of total investment in transport – is shown in Table II. This table also shows the gross earnings of the main-line railways as an indication of the resiliency of their revenues; a threefold expansion in ten years provided strong encouragement to investors to finance more railway-building in Canada. The final column, showing the rapid growth in value of the wheat

TABLE II *Investment in Transport, 1900–14*

	Gross investment*			
Year	Steam railways ($m.)	Highways, bridges, canals, harbours ($m.)	Gross earnings of main line railways† ($m.)	Value o, wheat crop ($m.)
1900	34·1	(6·0)	70·7	55·6
1901	38·9	6·9	72·9	85·3
1902	44·6	8·3	83·7	93·6
1903	55·9	9·9	96·1	78·5
1904	61·3	11·0	100·2	69·0
1905	75·2	12·0	106·5	106·1
1906	94·1	10·6	125·3	125·5
1907	136·5	17·5	146·7	93·1
1908	135·0	20·8	146·9	112·4
1909	131·0	22·5	145·1	166·7
1910	151·6	31·9	174·0	132·1
1911	170·7	42·1	188·7	230·9
1912	210·2	53·5	219·4	224·5
1913	232·4	65·1	256·7	231·7
1914	177·0	64·7	243·1	—

* Including replacement and repair (Buckley, op. cit. pp. 153–4).

† Year ending 30 June. Excludes government-owned railways and electric railways.

crop, provides a measure both of the pace of agricultural development and of the need for additional transport facilities.

Adding together fixed capital formation and exports and deducting imports (inclusive of invisibles as well as of commodity trade), we obtain (in Table III) what I have called above 'Gross Canadian Savings'.

The sum of exports and home investment increased in every year except 1904 and 1908; the same is true of imports. The changes in both totals (as shown in columns 4 and 5) kept step very closely, indicating (as we should expect) that savings maintained a relatively steady trend.

An inflationary impulse, then, coming from investment and exports raised money incomes in Canada at a rate dictated by the public's thrift and by its demand for imports. In real terms, what this meant was that the rising export and constructional

TABLE III *Investment, Savings, and Trade, 1900–14**

Year	Exports plus fixed capital formation ($m.)	Imports ($m.)	'Gross savings' ($m.)	Increase in col 1 ($m.)	Increase in col. 2 ($m.)
1900	361	234	127	—	—
1901	386	245	141	25	11
1902	462	276	196	76	31
1903	532	329	193	70	53
1904	511	328	187	−21	−1
1905	591	363	228	80	35
1906	728	429	299	137	66
1907	800	495	305	82	66
1908	743	440	303	−57	−55
1909	852	509	343	109	69
1910	954	623	331	102	114
1911	1071	729	342	117	106
1912	1265	889	347	194	160
1913	1376	951	425	111	78
1914	1135	805	330	−239	−146

* The figures for exports and imports in this table are those given by Professor F. A. Knox in 'Dominion Monetary Policy' (Appendix to the Report of the Royal Commission on Dominion Provincial Relations). They are revisions of estimates by Viner and include all current items, visible and invisible, except gold.

industries – notably agriculture and building – were bidding successfully in the labour market for immigrant and mobile labour, while the industries exposed to foreign competition in the Canadian market found it increasingly difficult, in the face of the resulting scarcity of labour and rising costs of production, to hold their own, even in an expanding market. There was a reorientation of the labour force away from consumption goods (which could be imported cheaply) and towards the constructional industries (which, backed by foreign loans, could afford to pay high wages); there was a further reorientation of labour away from foreign trade goods and towards domestic, non-traded goods.[1] These two changes were not distinct. They arose from the fact that many of the capital goods which Canada was in the process of acquiring had to be constructed on the spot. Canada could not import railway track, bridges, and houses. She could, and did, import men to do the work. The men were clothed with imported textiles, which would otherwise have gone to supply foreign markets. But had Canada wanted ships and locomotives only, they might have stayed at home and supplied their wants from much the same sources.

Symptomatic of the changed state of the labour market when investment was at its peak were the changes that took place in wages and in prices. We have seen that wages rose most in the 'domestic' industries and least in industries competing with imports. That this was true also of prices is well known from Professor Viner's work. The rise in domestic (wholesale) commodity prices between 1900 and 1913 was 61·7 per cent;[2] the rise in Coats's weighted index for all commodities was 31·9 per cent.[3] The explanation of this change is, I believe, twofold. First, the urgent demand for labour from the constructional trades put pressure on all industries either to raise wages or let labour go. The domestic industries were in a position to meet this pressure by raising wages. They had no foreign

[1] Cf. Viner, op. cit., pp. 262–3: 'It is difficult to explain the decline in the percentage of exports to total commodity production, without reference to the capital borrowings from abroad. Some of the relative decline in exports was undoubtedly due to the increasing extent to which Canadian raw materials were being manufactured in Canada for Canadian consumption, instead of being exported in their crude form in exchange for imported manufactured goods. But this increase in manufactures would not have been possible in nearly the same degree had it not been for the foreign investments of capital in Canadian manufacturing enterprises. The expansion of manufacturing not only absorbed an increased proportion of the Canadian production of raw materials, but it withdrew labour, from the production of raw materials which otherwise would have been exported, to the construction of plant and equipment and the fabrication, from imported raw materials, of manufactured commodities for domestic consumption. The development of roads, towns, and railroads, made possible by the borrowings abroad, absorbed a large part of the immigration of labour, and these consumed considerable quantities of Canadian commodities which would otherwise have been available for export.'

[2] Viner, op. cit., p. 230.

[3] *Cost of Living Report*, Vol. II, p. 23.

competition to face, and could raise prices without fear of a shrinkage in demand. The rapid increase in population, indeed, coupled with a rising standard of living, brought about a quite unprecedented expansion in the demand for domestic goods and services, in terms both of money and of real resources. On the side of supply, however, these goods could only be provided at increasing cost.[1] Manufacturers and imports, on the other hand, were supplied for the most part under conditions of decreasing cost. This divergent trend in (real) costs, like the divergent trend in wages, operated to widen the margin between domestic and other prices.[2]

There were, of course, other factors at work. The great rise in the earnings of domestic servants, for example, is probably to be associated with the comparative scarcity of women immigrants. The scarcity of wives and of domestic servants both arose from this, and each no doubt reinforced the other; where wives were scarce, domestic servants were in demand, and where servants were scarce, wives were in demand.

III *The Forces Governing Home Investment and Exports*

(*a*) AGRICULTURE: We have now to examine the forces which, in their turn, controlled home investment and exports. Over the period as a whole, the most important were the rise in agricultural prices in world markets and the opening-up of low-cost farming land and mineral deposits.[3] Even in the short period agriculture exercised a powerful influence alike on domestic purchasing power, borrowings abroad, and credit policy. A good harvest made it easy and profitable to borrow

[1] Two out of three of Viner's twenty-three 'domestic' commodities are agricultural products (op. cit., p. 230, n. 2).

[2] Cf. A. G. Silverman, 'The international trade of Great Britain, 1880–1913' (unpublished Ph.D. thesis in Harvard University Library), pp. 201–2: 'Because of perishability or large transportation costs, the sources of local supply are limited and apt to be subject to increasing costs. There is little incentive or opportunity for technical advance and improved organisation under such conditions. Competitive opportunities in other industries, in which the advantage is greater, means higher wages all round: and this further increases costs in the production of domestic commodities such as are included in [Viner's] index.'

[3] Viner, op. cit., pp. 261 et seq.; above, p. 159.

abroad, while the banks were less exacting in granting advances, and had larger resources out of which to lend. A harvest failure left people poorer and without the money or inclination to make capital extensions, while the banks, finding their reserves depleted because of an unfavourable balance of payments, pursued a policy of caution. The excellent harvest of 1901 and 1902 sent up exports and investment in those years and (even more) in 1903.[1] The comparatively disappointing harvest of 1903, followed by the still shorter crop of 1904, brought about a minor recession of business, which lasted until the beginning of 1905. In that year, crops and business activity moved up together, the arable area being greatly extended in the meantime to take advantage of the high prices offered for grain.[2] In 1906 and 1907 harvests were poor and investment fell off. In 1908 the crops, with the exception of wheat and pastures, were rather better, and as prices rose far above normal, agricultural exports fetched higher values than in 1907 and investment began to recover.[3] The succeeding years, with the outstanding exception of 1910, saw a series of bountiful harvests which came to an end only in 1914. Investment, financed largely from abroad, was on a correspondingly ample scale, and, supported by the government's expansionist policy of railway-building, and by the encouraging steadiness of grain prices, was able to surmount the harvest failure of 1910 without difficulty.

(*b*) FOREIGN BORROWING AND BANKING POLICY: We come at last to investment by foreigners and banking policy. What part did they play?

Investment by foreigners sustained 'home investment' at a level beyond the savings of Canadian citizens. Had foreigners been less willing to embark their capital in Canadian enterprises, 'home investment' would have been undertaken on a less ambitious scale, the pressure on the labour market would

---

[1] It should be remembered that the export statistics of any calendar year reflect the state of the crops both in that year *and* in the preceding one.

[2] Wheat prices in Canada rose sharply in 1904 under the influence of two successive short crops in the United States.

[3] 1908 was a year of famine in India.

have been reduced, and Canadians would have been able to supply more of their own requirements instead of importing goods from abroad. Any reduction in investment in Canada tended to make the balance of payments more favourable: directly, by curtailing imports of capital goods; and indirectly, by freeing labour for the production of traded goods. It also reduced the volume of employment by checking the inflow of migrants, and, in the short period, by throwing men out of work. In this way the demand for traded goods fell, while the supply tended to increase; a reduction in investment led first to a reduction in imports of all kinds, and later – although this was not a *necessary* consequence – to a rise in exports. Home investment – as determined largely by foreign borrowing – governed the balance of payments.

There was, however, no guarantee that the balance of payments and foreign borrowings would move evenly up or down, or that the transfer of capital would take place smoothly. Equilibrium was, in point of fact, preserved by the Canadian banks. Banking policy was important in two ways. First, in the absence of any organized bill market in Canada, the proceeds of loans issued abroad were transferred to Canada through the agency of the Canadian banks. The banks held large reserves in foreign centres (mainly in New York), and the primary effect of an increase in foreign borrowing and a bigger loan transfer than usual was to add to these reserves. The Canadian banks lent abroad what foreigners lent to Canada. The balance of payments remained unchanged and the real transfer was postponed. In short, the Canadian banks, being practically the sole dealers in foreign exchange, maintained a steady price for it by adding to their stock or allowing it to run down according as there was a surplus or shortage arising from commercial and loan transactions. Their secondary reserves[1] took the place of gold as the residual item in the balance of payments.[2]

[1] That is, call loans elsewhere than in Canada and net balances due from banks outside Canada. The proportion of *cash* reserves to demand liabilities was kept relatively steady.

[2] Although *loans* on short-term were not made abroad by other Canadian bodies, there was some *borrowing* on short-term by Canadian governments and

In the second place, the Canadian banks pursued a loan policy calculated to keep fluctuations in their secondary reserves within limits. It has been suggested that the banks played a purely passive role, and refused 'no deserving request for an extension of credit'.[1] This is as hard to believe of a group of banks as it is of a single bank. No bank can maintain an inflexible conception of what is 'deserving' when its reserves are slipping away. There would be no sense in the repeated complaints of monetary stringency in 1907 and 1913 if 'deserving' borrowers were not finding it difficult to arrange credits. The builders who were reported in 1913 to be using their own savings to pay for work on dwelling-houses in the suburbs of Montreal[2] were hardly less credit-worthy than those who had no difficulty in raising money six months earlier. Nevertheless, it is clear that circumstances might give an *appearance* of passiveness to the behaviour of the banks. Since a favourable balance was normally accompanied by a rise in investment, the demand for credit and the secondary reserves of the banks tended to move upwards together; so that it becomes difficult to disentangle changes in credit policy from changes in the demand for loans in the recorded statistics of bank advances.

Banking policy exerted a double influence on the money supply. First, the banks did not offset an increase in their foreign assets (such as was brought about by an increase in foreign borrowing) by a decrease in their domestic assets. Any acquisition of funds for transfer to Canada, therefore, increased the banks' foreign assets and domestic liabilities simultaneously. An increase in investment financed from abroad meant an

---

private corporations – especially in 1912–13. This borrowing – and the arranging of short-term credits with British financial institutions or manufacturing companies – can also be regarded as an equilibrating factor in the balance of payments. But it was never, so far as I am aware, of more than minor importance (cf. Viner, op. cit., p. 122). It should also be noted that call loans in New York made directly from the Canadian head offices of banks without agencies in New York are reported as call loans in Canada and are not included, therefore, in secondary reserves (Viner, *Studies in the Theory of International Trade*, p. 432).

[1] 'There is abundant evidence . . . that (the banks) neither contracted nor expanded their current loans primarily because of the state of their cash reserves' (Viner, op. cit., p. 176).

[2] Canadian *Labour Gazette*, May 1913, p. 1182.

automatic expansion in the money supply in Canada. The increased in investment, reinforced by the expansion in the money supply, drove up money incomes and prices and helped to turn the balance of payments against Canada, causing the secondary reserves of the banks to return towards their former level. This was the first way in which fluctuations in the secondary reserves of the banks were kept within limits.

Secondly, the banks were able to affect investment and the

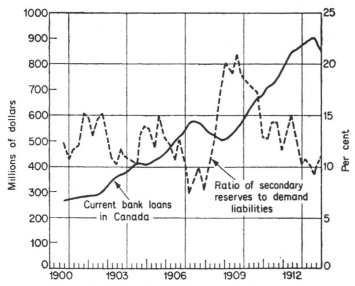

CHART 3. Current bank loans in Canada and secondary reserves, 1900–13.

balance of payments in a more direct manner by extending credit more freely whenever their secondary reserves increased.[1] Chart 3 shows fairly conclusively that changes in bank advances responded to the changes in secondary reserves at a rather earlier date. The most important exception is the year 1910, when the banks, out of the abundance of their secondary reserves, maintained easy terms of credit and helped to keep up home investment when poor crop conditions might have caused a setback.[2]

The control of credit by the banks gave them power to check

[1] The assets of the banks in Canada other than advances rose comparatively smoothly throughout.

[2] Cf. above, p. 168.

or encourage home investment. Whenever foreign borrowings were not inflating home investment fast enough to bring about a real transfer, the banks were forced at first to take up the difference in foreign lending or in gold imports. They could then use their power over home investment, relaxing the terms of credit until their secondary reserves were at a lower, more satisfactory level, and the original increase in foreign lending had passed over into home investment. The more complaisant they were in large swings in their secondary reserves, the less violently did they require to modify the terms of credit. Had they sought to keep secondary reserves constant, they would have forced correspondingly wide fluctuations on Canadian investment and money incomes. The fact that secondary reserves were allowed to swing between less than 8 and over 20 per cent of demand liabilities in Canada suggests that, on the whole, credit policy operated to dampen rather than to aggravate these fluctuations.

Whatever the mechanism by which foreign borrowing was translated into investment in Canada, it was governed both by the domestic circumstances that made investment attractive and by the circumstances abroad that made the raising of capital there a practicable operation. Within Canada circumstances remained favourable throughout nearly the whole of the period. The opening up of the west offered a good return to the farmer if he had adequate transport and labour; it offered a good return to the railways if they could raise capital at low rates of interest and hire the men to build the permanent way; it offered a good return to the immigrant, discontented with a low and apparently stationary standard of living; and it had the backing of the government, which was anxious to accelerate the whole operation. The expenditure of borrowed funds itself generated an inflation that made investment still more profitable and attractive; the arrival of immigrants in need of housing gave an additional impulse to construction. But everything rested on two props: the continued inflow of foreign capital and the continuance of market conditions favourable to Canadian exports. With the London capital market strained to the uttermost, it was inevitable that one of the props should wobble a little now and then; and with the double risk of short crops and a setback in agricultural prices the other, in a community so dependent on the export of primary produce, was not altogether secure.

The magnitudes involved in foreign investment in Canada are shown in Table IV. These are of interest mainly as showing

TABLE IV *Foreign Borrowing and Trade, 1900–14**

Year	Net long-term capital movement into Canada ($m.)	Debit balance on current account ($m.)	Commodity exports ($m.)	Commodity imports ($m.)	Terms of trade (1900–4 = 100)
1900	29·8	36·6	156·0	176·5	92·4
1901	35·1	23·1	170·2	182·6	99·9
1902	40·3	32·0	190·4	203·4	103·5
1903	51·7	74·1	201·9	251·8	101·5
1904	58·9	97·5	176·1	249·2	102·7
1905	109·5	87·3	205·2	263·6	102·2
1906	102·3	102·0	254·0	312·3	95·3
1907	91·1	166·9	253·8	363·0	95·9
1908	218·1	134·4	249·3	282·6	116·6
1909	249·4	158·3	269·0	339·6	118·0
1910	308·2	251·3	280·8	429·0	112·8
1911	343·4	363·7	284·1	506·3	113·2
1912	316·1	421·3	351·7	626·0	110·7
1913	541·7	408·2	442·9	654·9	106·1
1914	320·6	288·2	369·1	470·8	—

* The estimates in cols. 1–4 are taken from F. A. Knox, *Dominion Monetary Policy*, and are based on those of Viner. The debit balance on current account includes the balance of trade in gold. The estimates in col. 5 are calculated from the indices of export and import prices in Table VI (below, p. 183).

how little the process of expansion was interrupted even by the external factors. But they also put in a rather clearer light the connection between foreign investment and the terms of trade. There was a time when the causal connection was traced from the first of these to the second. But the evidence points in the reverse direction. It was *after* the terms of trade moved to Canada's advantage that the main bursts of investment in Canada occurred. If it had been impossible to borrow abroad, these improvements might not have been sustained; the changes in investment and in the terms of trade were wrapped up together in the whole process of expansion. But it is certainly misleading, if the two things have to be isolated and a causal sequence established between them, to argue as if the experience of Canada showed that capital transfer *provoked* a favourable change in the terms of trade.

IV *The Fluctuations in Investment*

We can now give a brief sketch of the fluctuations that did take place between 1900 and 1913 – the 'interruptions' of which we spoke above.[1]

The expansion in Canadian trade and investment that began in 1900 received no check until late in 1903. The depression which set in towards the end of that year can be traced to a combination of circumstances of which the chief were a comparatively poor harvest, a severe winter, and a slump in the United States. In 1904 exports fell off, the rise in investment slackened, and imports marked time. In the labour market there were reports of unemployment among unskilled workers in nearly all the provinces,[2] and immigration was less active. Wages ceased to rise. On the capital market, interest rates were higher[3] and although the building industry was very busy in the west, there was a reduction in building in Montreal, Quebec, Hamilton, and other towns in the east.[4] The banks whose secondary reserves had been falling since August 1902,[5] began to lend less freely in the second quarter of 1904. Between April 1904 and February 1905, advances rose only

---

[1] P. 160.   [2] Canadian *Labour Gazette*, January 1905.

[3] Cf. the yield of city mortgages (Table VIII, below). The rise in interest rates reflected the restriction of credit by the banks.

[4] In the spring of 1904 it was reported from Winnipeg that 'employment agencies were literally besieged with applicants for employment. Large contributions to the ranks of the unemployed came from the camps, and there was a very observable influx from the United States' (Canadian *Labour Gazette*, April 1904, p. 1114). But by the summer, there were boom conditions here and at Calgary, Edmonton, and Vancouver.

[5] Secondary reserves fell from a high point of $70·8 million in August 1902 to $42·2 million in April 1903; from this low level they recovered to $55·4 million in September 1903, but by April 1904 were down again to $40·7 million. These movements were partly seasonal.

$5 million as compared with an increase of $36 million between April 1903 and February 1904. After April 1904, however, secondary reserves rose very quickly, partly, no doubt, because of credit restriction, but partly also because of heavy borrowings abroad. In 1905 investment, exports, immigration, wages, bank advances, etc., all resumed their upward course.

The depression of 1904 was a brief affair – little more than a spell of dull trade. It originated in the export industries and had no serious repercussions on investment. The slump of 1907–8 was more complicated in origin. Exports in 1907 were up to the level of the preceding year; but they failed to increase, in spite of fetching higher prices. At the same time, foreign borrowing was becoming more difficult because of the tightness of money in London and Wall Street. Thus home investment which continued to increase in 1907, began to outrun foreign borrowings and to deplete the secondary reserves of the Canadian banks. This forced on the banks a deflationary policy which reacted seriously on investment and proved only too successful in restoring equilibrium to the balance of payments.

The net foreign assets of the banks began to decline in the last quarter of 1906;[1] in the first quarter of 1907 the decline was carried farther, and secondary reserves fell below 8 per cent of demand liabilities in Canada (compared with a previous minimum of 10 per cent in June 1904). After April, bank advances ceased to expand, and by the end of the year had fallen by $30 million. In June it was reported that money was tight 'owing to delayed deliveries of the western crop of 1906'.[2] But in July and later months, when the 1906 crop had long been delivered, complaints continued to be made. Tight money was holding up building in the west as early as July.[3] By October, the east felt the same influence.[4]

[1] This is not shown in the statistics of secondary reserves (for quarterly data, see Viner, op. cit., pp. 166–7). There was a sharp increase in 'deposits elsewhere than in Canada' (which are not included in secondary reserves) and no compensating increase in foreign assets.

[2] Canadian *Labour Gazette*, June 1907, p. 1321.

[3] Canadian *Labour Gazette*, July 1907, p. 9; August 1907, p. 115; September 1907, p. 283.

[4] Canadian *Labour Gazette*, October 1907, p. 354. High building costs were also blamed. For mortgage rates, see Table VIII.

The harvest of 1907 happened to be rather a poor one. Exports of lumber and raw materials, moreover, were hit by the slump in the two chief markets for Canadian exports – Great Britain and the United States. No relief to the stringency of credit could be expected, therefore, from the favourable repercussions of an increase in exports. Instead, the export situation created an atmosphere still more unfavourable to investment. There was less traffic on the railways, operating expenses were as high as ever, and net earnings were falling. The fall in building construction, therefore, tended to be reinforced by a fall in railway construction.[1] Immigration, wages, and imports all fell in sympathy.

By the middle of 1908, prospects were much better. Secondary reserves had been rising gradually for some months; in the second half of the year they nearly doubled. Foreign borrowing was on a larger scale than ever, and whereas imports fell heavily to meet the reduction in investment and employment, exports remained steady. Interest rates and costs were both lower, and harvest reports were favourable. Bank advances, however, continued to fall until February 1909, and apart from railway construction in the west (e.g. on the Grand Trunk Pacific)[2] investment was also on the decline.

The first signs of recovery were observable in the autumn of 1908. The building permits passed at Winnipeg, for example, were well up on the 1907 figures in the second half of 1908.[3] In the east, manufacturing industry was reported to be showing an improvement towards the end of the year. By 1909 recovery was well under way.

---

[1] The part played by high building costs was also important.

[2] This line had the backing of government guarantees; the decision to proceed with construction was not governed simply by economic considerations.

[3] The value of building permits in each half-year was (in $m.):

	1st half-year	2nd half-year
1906	7·1	5·7
1907	4·4	2·0
1908	2·2	3·3
1909	5·5	3·8
1910	9·9	5·2

See Canadian *Labour Gazette*, August 1910, p. 177.

The final depression had little connection with exports. Export prices, it is true, fell – and fell heavily – in 1913. But export *values* were well up on 1912. Again we must look to the 'financial stringency', of which the west was complaining in February and the east a few months later, for an explanation of the depression. The financial stringency followed a great reduction in secondary reserves in the second half of 1912.[1] Home investment was again outrunning foreign borrowing, and forcing the banking system to restrict credit. Advances did not actually fall until the last two months of 1913; but the brake seems to have been put on as early as October 1912. In the year from October 1912 to October 1913, the increase in advances was no more than $25 million, compared with an increase of over $110 million in the preceding year.

As in the slump of 1907–8, it was building activity which proved most sensitive to rising interest rates and credit control. The builders who, in Montreal, were predicting a record year in April were being forced in May to abandon plans for the construction of 'several large buildings', mainly because of dear money.[2] The fall in building activity and in other forms of investment operated to reduce imports and maintain the secondary reserves of the banks. By 1914 the course of events in 1908 was being repeated on a bigger scale than before. But the autumn of that year, unlike the autumn of 1908, brought no promise that the slump would reach a normal end.

V *The 'Smoothness' of the Capital Transfer*

There is one final point which I should like to discuss. It is often said that the transfer of capital to Canada took place 'smoothly'. What this means is not too easy to understand. If it means: without an excessive rise in prices, who is to say what is excessive and what is not? If it means: without large movements of gold, the explanation of the smoothness of the transfer is that the Canadian banks preferred to vary their holdings of more profitable assets – loans at call to the New York money

---

[1] There was a fall from $170·4 million in June to $123·3 million in December.

[2] Canadian *Labour Gazette*, April 1913, p. 1052; May 1913, p. 1182.

market; and that they were willing to allow these 'secondary' reserves to vary within wide limits. If it means, finally: without causing disturbance to trade and employment, the answer is that there was in fact a good deal of disturbance and un-employment.

Nevertheless, it may be admitted that, in comparison with the transfer of capital in the inter-war years, investment in Canada took place with surprising smoothness in all of these senses. Why was this?

First, it was accompanied by a *labour* transfer on an equally enormous scale. Immigration and investment fluctuated closely with one another; so that, for example, whenever a railway was being built, foreign countries furnished the men as well as the capital. They also furnished much of the railway material. The result was to limit the pressure on Canadian labour to adapt itself to the new situation: much as the migra-tion of Scottish workers to England to help in the construction of Scottish-owned railways would facilitate the transfer of capital.

Secondly, the transfer was smoothed out by the credit policy of the Canadian banks. Sudden changes in foreign borrowings were offset by equal changes in the loans of the banks in foreign money markets. The banks thus acted as a buffer and steadied the real transfer of capital.

Thirdly, it must not be overlooked that the whole period was one of rapid expansion with an undercurrent of optimistic expectations. It was easy for a country to make adjustments so long as prices kept rising and the demand for labour was keen. Those who could not make a profit or find a job in one trade had no difficulty in moving to a more hopeful line of business. Recessions in business activity were short, and due more to rashness and over-hastiness than to any deficiency of profitable opportunities for investment. All this was true not only of Canada but of all other countries. The stresses and strains of capital transfer were far more readily borne in an adaptable world of rising prices and rising profits than in one with a background of falling prices, business losses, and chronic unemployment.

Put rather differently, the adjustments that Canada had to make were to a steadily expanding volume of foreign borrowing. There were no abrupt transitions from a debit to a credit balance of payments; in 1907–8, for example, foreign investment in Canada was not lower than in earlier years, but far higher. But, as everyone knows, it is impossible to go on indefinitely making all the adjustments in one direction; there comes a day of reckoning to the confirmed debtor when the source of funds dries up or when – still worse – repayment is demanded, more often than not at a most inconvenient moment. It is the shudder of an economy under *that* tremendous impact which makes capital transfer so stormy a passage, not the tackings this way and that under a fair inflationary wind.

Finally, investment before the First World War *was* investment, and not just a swop of one kind of money or security for another. When Canada borrowed, she did so with a view to increasing her stock of capital instruments, and of hiring labour or buying equipment to assist in the work of construction. She invested what she borrowed. And, as we have seen, an increase in investment has a powerful effect on the balance of payments. The two cannot readily move far out of line with one another. Thus the fact that it was a genuine capital transfer (as defined in the opening paragraph of this essay), and not a new-fangled pseudo-capital transfer, contributed as much as anything to make the transfer take place so smoothly.

STATISTICAL APPENDIX

Wages

I have used a wage index which differs considerably from the index of weekly wages constructed by Coats[1] and used by Viner. In Britain, net increases or decreases in weekly wages, as reported by the Board of Trade,[2] moved in close correspondence with available indices of money wages. It is reasonable to apply the same principle to Canada, where, between 1903 and

[1] *Cost of Living Report*, Vol. II, p. 427.
[2] In its *Annual Reports on Changes in Wages and Hours of Labour*.

1913, the Department of Labour published statistics of increases and decreases in weekly earnings in a large number of trades.

Accordingly, I have adopted Coats's weighted index number weekly wages for the years 1900–2 and 1913 and interpolated

TABLE V *Wages and the Cost of Living, 1900–13*

Year	Wages in all industries*	Wages in all industries†	Cost of living‡	Wholesale prices§
1900	100·0	100·0	100	100·0
1901	101·6	101·6	—	100·2
1902	103·8	103·8	—	103·6
1903	108·4	106·5	—	103·7
1904	108·8	109·3	—	104·5
1905	109·9	113·1	110	107·6
1906	119·5	116·5	—	113·5
1907	127·0	122·6	—	122·1
1908	121·6	124·8	—	118·2
1909	125·6	129·0	125	119·4
1910	130·2	134·0	129·9	121·0
1911	135·8	137·9	133·8	123·9
1912	142·5	145·0	140·9	136·0
1913	148·9	148·9	142·9	131·9

* Figures for 1900–2 and for 1913 taken from *Cost of Living Report*, Vol. II, p. 431. Others interpolated on basis of net changes in weekly earnings of which the Department of Labour had record.

† Alternative estimate from *Cost of Living Report*, Vol. II, p. 431.

‡ *Cost of Living Report*, Vol. II, p. 435. Cost of living in December of each year for a working class family of five, spending 20 per cent of its budget on house rent.

§ *Cost of Living Report*, Vol. II, p. 22. Converted to a 1900 base by Viner, op. cit., p. 220.

on the basis of the Department of Labour's statistics.[1] The same procedure has been repeated for the wages of unskilled labour and of building workers. The indices obtained in this way are in agreement with the reports published from time to time in the Canadian *Labour Gazette* on the state of the labour market,[2] with the fluctuations that took place in the note issue, and so on.

On the other hand, they diverge in some years, e.g. 1904 and 1908, from Coats's index of weekly wages. It is quite clear that these were bad years in which some setback in money

[1] As given in the *Cost of Living Report*, Vol. II, p. 424.

[2] As summarized in the *Cost of Living Report*, Vol. II, pp. 418 et seq.

wages is likely to have taken place. Coats's index, however, shows an almost uninterrupted rise. It is also difficult to reconcile the figures for wage-cuts and wage-advances with the figures for average weekly wage-rates. One set of figures shows a large reduction in wages in lumbering in 1908; the other a rise. One shows wages in the building industry rising sharply in 1903, the other in 1904. I think the figures of wage-cuts and wage-advances the more plausible of the two.

Cost of Living

I have used Coats's estimate of the increase in the weekly expenditure on foodstuffs, fuel and rent of a family of five with an income of $872 in 1900. This shows a rise in the cost of living between 1900 and 1913 of 42·9 per cent. For the retail cost of foodstuffs Coats estimates the increase at 41·5 per cent, for fuel at 25·4 per cent, and for working-class rents at 61·7 per cent. The index for foodstuffs is unsatisfactory and may slightly understate the rise. The rise in rents may also be a little on the low side. On the other hand, Coats omits some items such as imported manufactures (including clothing) and services like railway transport, electric lighting, water supply and so on, which either rose comparatively little, or fell in price (electric light fell by nearly 30 per cent).

Wholesale Prices

Viner's index of domestic commodity prices is an unweighted average for twenty-three products, of which two out of three are agricultural products such as potatoes, milk, hay, and strawberries (op. cit., p. 230, note 2). Since these products are liable to erratic fluctuations in supply and price, the index is not altogether satisfactory; but it probably reflects with fair accuracy the changes which we know to have taken place. It agrees closely, for example, with Coats's index of house rents, which usually reflect the trend in domestic commodity prices. I have, therefore, used Viner's index without change. For most purposes, however, it is preferable to use a 1900–4 rather than a 1900 base (cf. Silverman, op. cit., p. 258) as the fluctuations in prices between 1900 and 1902 were peculiarly erratic.

For export prices, Viner gives three different indices (op. cit., p. 233). In the first, exports are weighted according to importance in 1900–4; in the second, according to importance in 1913; the third is unweighted. In the first index, the twenty-one most important commodities of export in 1900–4 are weighted by (1) dividing them into three groups of two, four, and fifteen commodities, so that each group represents an approximately equal value of exports; (2) constructing a price-index for each group; and (3) taking an average of the three price-indices. The second index is constructed on similar lines for the twenty-two most important articles of export in 1913.

These three methods of weighting yield results between which there is surprisingly little agreement. No one method, moreover, can claim superiority over the others. I have been driven to use yet a fourth method – one which is rather complicated but which offers a commonsense way out of the difficulty.

I have started from the weighted price-indices for groups of export commodities given by Viner in a later chapter (op. cit., pp. 265, 270). By inspection, the main changes in weights took place very quickly between 1906 and 1908; a second rapid change took place in 1912–13. That is, in the periods 1900–5 and 1908–11 weights did not change greatly. First, therefore, I have weighted exports according to the importance of each of Viner's groups in 1900–5 and calculated an index of export prices for the period 1900–8. Next, I have used the weights appropriate to the years 1908–11 to construct an index for the period 1905–13. For the years where there two indices overlap I have taken the average of the proportionate changes. The final index represents a fair compromise between the indices constructed by Professor Viner.

The calculations of an index number of import prices is a more difficult proposition. The index used by Viner takes no account of imports of manufactured goods, although these formed nearly two-thirds of total imports. In particular, Viner uses no indices of the price of textile manufactures. As textiles were imported almost exclusively from Great Britain we can

TABLE VI *Export and Import Prices, 1900–13*

Year	Domestic prices	Export prices (weighted according to importance in 1900–5)	Export prices (weighted according to importance in 1908–11)	Index of export prices*	Index of import prices†
1900	100·0	100·0	—	100·0	100·0
1901	111·5	101·6	—	101·6	94·0
1902	118·5	103·3	—	103·3	92·2
1903	119·1	105·0	—	105·0	95·7
1904	119·1	103·0	—	103·0	92·7
1905	120·9	108·2	86·3	108·2	97·8
1906	122·8	114·0	88·2	112·1	108·7
1907	135·6	120·5	96·1	119·9	115·6
1908	133·6	121·2	98·7	122·2	96·8
1909	141·0	122·5	100·2	124·0	97·1
1910	145·7	—	100·9	124·9	102·3
1911	151·4	—	100·1	126·0	101·1
1912	161·8	—	104·5	129·4	108·0
1913	161·7	—	101·8	126·0	109·7

* In calculating this index each of the price indices for the subgroups of exports has been converted to a base of 1908–11 = 100. It is assumed that the weighting assigned to the commodities in each subgroup did not alter greatly between 1900 and 1908–11.

† Using the following weights: textiles 2, iron and steel manufactures, 4, raw materials 2, foodstuffs 1.

cover this group of imports by using Silverman's index of the price of British textile exports.[1] For manufactures of iron and steel I have used an index of metal prices in the U.S.A., which supplied Canada with practically all of its iron and steel imports.[2] In addition, I have used the indices of the prices of imported foodstuffs and raw materials calculated by Viner (op. cit., p. 236). The heavy weighting – two-thirds – given to metals and raw materials may exaggerate the violence of the fluctuations that took place in import prices.

The index number which this calculation yields does not differ greatly from the one constructed by Viner. It shows a

[1] A. G. Silverman, 'Monthly index numbers of British export and import prices, 1880–1913', *Rev. Econ. Statist.* 1930.

[2] This index is an unweighted average for forty-four iron and steel products published in *Bulletin* no. 181 of the Bureau of Labor Statistics, U.S. Department of Labor.

rise of less than 10 per cent between 1900 and 1913, compared with a rise of 14 per cent in Viner's index.

Migration

In Chart 2 I have used the official statistics of immigration and Viner's estimates of emigration.

That these figures underestimate the balance of immigration into Canada is readily demonstrated. The population of Canada increased between 1 June 1901 and 1 June 1911 by 1,835,000. The birth-rate in 1901 was approximately 27 per 1,000 (at the time of the census there were 24·5 children of under 1 year per 1,000 of the population). The deathrate in 1911 was approximately 14 per 1,000 (Viner, op. cit., p. 48), and in 1901 was at least as great (e.g. the proportion of the population over 60 was much higher). The natural increase was thus at most 13 per 1,000, or 70,000 in 1901 and 93,000 in 1911. The aggregate natural increase was, say, 800,000 over the ten-year period; and the net gain by immigration must, therefore, have been at least 1 million as compared with about 650,000 in the estimates which I have used above.

TABLE VII *Immigration into Canada, 1900–13*

Year	Immigrant arrivals*	Saloon immigrants†	Total	Emigration from Canada‡	Net balance of migration
1900	41,681	2,537	44,218	20,937	23,281
1901	55,747	3,338	59,085	21,196	37,889
1902	89,102	3,660	92,762	34,279	58,483
1903	138,660	4,397	143,057	45,101	97,956
1904	131,252	4,414	135,666	61,807	73,859
1905	141,465	4,882	146,347	82,376	63,971
1906	211,653	5,977	217,630	113,731	103,899
1907	272,409	7,436	279,845	152,467	127,378
1908	143,326	5,164	148,490	209,752	−61,262
1909	173,694	4,174	177,868	187,400	−9,532
1910	286,839	3,311	290,150	190,286	99,864
1911	331,288	3,715	335,003	198,537	136,466
1912	375,756	3,526	379,282	209,458	169,824
1913	400,870	3,614	404,484	225,392	179,092

* *Canada Year Book*, 1936, p. 186.
† Viner, op. cit., p. 46.
‡ Viner, op. cit., p. 57.

An alternative estimate of the natural increase is obtained by deducting the estimated number of deaths, plus the number of children entering Canada as immigrants, from the total number of children less than 10 years of age in Canada at 1 June 1911. This also points to a figure of rather less than 800,000 for the ten-year period.

Finance

In Table VIII are reproduced some of the more important statistics relevant to a discussion of monetary policy over the period. The annual increase in the note issue throws light on

TABLE VIII. *Money and Credit in Canada, 1900–13*

	Increase in cash in hands of public* ($m.)	Increase in secondary reserves of banks† ($m.)	Increase in net foreign assets of the banks‡ ($m.)	Increase in bank advances§ ($m.)	Yield on city mortgages‖ (1900 = 100)
1900	5·9	—	—	—	100·0
1901	4·6	19·4	20·5	13·6	100·5
1902	5·7	0·9	−3·0	33·7	100·3
1903	6·0	−7·5	−20·2	61·5	100·8
1904	1·9	22·8	17·1	29·4	102·0
1905	2·7	3·0	11·4	44·6	99·7
1906	8·2	−5·6	−20·2	90·3	102·5
1907	6·5	−21·6	−24·3	−7·9	108·6
1908	−5·1	90·8	84·7	−44·8	106·1
1909	3·1	22·7	24·2	80·9	107·2
1910	10·2	−41·2	−36·4	84·4	109·8
1911	9·8	5·6	−28·4	97·8	111·0
1912	13·3	−5·4	−9·0	106·4	114·7
1913	11·0	6·5	12·6	−25·3	121·2

* Increase in average monthly circulation of the notes of the Chartered Banks and of Dominion Notes of $1, $2, $4, and $5.

† Increase in call loans elsewhere than in Canada and net balances due from banks outside Canada.

‡ Net foreign assets are taken to be net balances due from abroad plus current and call loans elsewhere than in Canada, less deposits elsewhere than in Canada.

§ Increase in current loans in Canada of Canadian Chartered Banks between 31 December and 31 December. Current loans in Canada and elsewhere were not separately distinguished before July 1900. The increase in advances in 1900 may have been about £15 million.

‖ Index number (weighted by population of cities) of interest on loans secured by first mortgages on city house property (*Cost of Living Report*, Vol. II, p. 724).

changes in wage incomes. The annual increase in the 'second-ary' reserves of the banks helps to explain their inflationary or deflationary bias. The state of the balance of payments is shown in the changes taking place in the net foreign assets of the bank. The annual change in bank advances is a measure of the rate at which the banking system was expanding or con-tracting credit. The yield on city mortgages is an index both of the cost of raising capital in the building industry, and of the ease or difficulty with which a mortgage could be arranged at the current rate.

Select Bibliography

References to most of the important books and articles relevant to the discussion of British capital exports between 1870 and 1914 are cited by one or other of the authors included above. This bibliography will therefore be very selective. It virtually ignores the large literature on short-term international capital movements during this period.

I *The General Setting*

BROWN, A. J. 'Britain and the World Economy', *Yorkshire Bulletin of Economic and Social Research* (1965).

CAIRNCROSS, A. K. *Home and Foreign Investment 1870–1913* (1953).

FEIS, H. *Europe the World's Banker 1870–1914* (1930).

HOBSON, C. K. *The Export of Capital* (1914).

IMLAH, A. H. *Economic Elements in the Pax Britannica* (1958).

JENKS, L. H. *The Migration of British Capital to 1875* (2nd ed. 1963).

KAHN, A. E. *Great Britain in the World Economy* (1946).

LANDES, DAVID S. 'Technological Change and Development in Western Europe 1750–1914', in H. J. Habakkuk and M. Postan (eds.), *The Cambridge Economic History of Europe*, Vol. VI (1965).

ROSTOW, W. W. *The British Economy of the Nineteenth Century* (1948).

THOMAS, B. *Migration and Economic Growth* (1954).

II *Experience of Areas of Recent Settlement*

(a) *Argentina*

FERNS, H. S. *Britain and Argentina in the Nineteenth Century* (1960).

FORD, A. G. *The Gold Standard 1880–1914. Britain and Argentina* (1962).

JOSLIN, D. *A Century of Banking in Latin America. Bank of London and South America Ltd. 1862–1962* (1963).

RIPPY, J. F. *British Investments in Latin America 1822–1949* (1959).

WILLIAMS, J. H. *Argentine International Trade under Inconvertible Paper Money 1880–1900* (1920).

(b) *Australia*

BAILEY, J. D. *Growth and Depression. Contrasts in the Australian and British Economies, 1870–1914* (1956).

BAILEY, J. D. *A Hundred Years of Pastoral Banking. A History of the Australian Mercantile Land and Finance Company 1863–1963* (1966).

BUTLIN, N. G. *Investment in Australian Economic Development 1861–1900* (1964).

BUTLIN, S. J. *Australia and New Zealand Bank. The Bank of Australasia and the Union Bank of Australia 1828–1951* (1961).

HALL, A. R. *The London Capital Market and Australia 1870–1914* (1963).

(c) *Canada*

BUCKLEY, K. *Capital Formation in Canada 1896–1930* (1955).

HARTLAND, P. 'Canadian Balance of Payments since 1868', in *Trends in the American Economy in the Nineteenth Century.* Studies in Income and Wealth, Vol. XXIV (1960).

STOVEL, J. A. *Canada in the World Economy* (1959).

VINER, J. *Canada's Balance of International Indebtedness 1900–1913* (1924).

(d) *New Zealand*

SIMKIN, C. S. F. *The Instability of a Dependent Economy. Economic Fluctuations in New Zealand 1840–1914* (1951).

(e) *United States of America*

HIDY, R. W. *The House of Baring in American Trade and Finance* (1949).

SIMON, M. 'The United States Balance of Payments, 1861–1900', in *Trends in the American Economy in the Nineteenth Century*. Studies in Income and Wealth, Vol. XXIV (1960).

SPENCE, C. C. *British Investments and the American Mining Frontier, 1860–1901* (1958).

WILLIAMSON, J. G. *American Growth and the Balance of Payments, 1820–1913* (1964).

III *Other Regions*

(a) *Africa*

DUNCAN, A. J. 'South African Capital Imports 1893–1898', *Canadian Journal of Political and Economic Science* (1948).

FRANKEL, S. H. *Capital Investment in Africa* (1938).

LANDES, DAVID S. *Bankers and Pashas. International Finance and Economic Imperialism in Egypt* (1958).

(b) *Asia*

HOU, CHI-MING. *Foreign Investment and Economic Development in China, 1840–1937* (1965).

MACPHERSON, W. J. 'Investment in Indian Railways, 1845–1875', *Economic History Review* (1955).

PANDIT, Y. S. *India's Balance of Payments* (1937).

RAMACHANDRAN, N. *Foreign Plantation Investment in Ceylon 1889–1958* (1963).

SAN, E-TU ZEU. *Chinese Railways and British Interests 1898–1911* (1954).

THORNER, D. 'Great Britain and the Development of India's Railways', *Journal of Economic History* (1951).

IV *Some Special Aspects*

ABRAMOVITZ, M. 'The Nature and Significance of Kuznets Cycles', *Economic Development and Cultural Change* (1961).

GOTTLIEB, M. *Estimates of Residential Building, United States, 1840–1939* (1964).

LEWIS, J. PARRY. *Building Cycles and Britain's Growth* (1965).

MARTIN, K. 'Capital Movements, the Terms of Trade and the

Balance of Payments', *Bulletin of the Oxford Institute of Statistics* 1949.

MATTHEWS, R. C. O. *The Trade Cycle* (1959).

TINBERGEN, J. *Business Cycles in the United Kingdom 1870–1914* (1951).

WILSON, R. *Capital Imports and the Terms of Trade* (1931).

For Product Safety Concerns and Information please contact our EU
representative GPSR@taylorandfrancis.com Taylor & Francis Verlag GmbH,
Kaufingerstraße 24, 80331 München, Germany

Printed and bound by CPI Group (UK) Ltd, Croydon, CR0 4YY
01/05/2025
01858447-0001